PRIORITY MAIL

PAM & STAN CAMPBELL

PRIORITY MAIL

VICTOR BOOKS®

A DIVISION OF SCRIPTURE PRESS PUBLICATIONS INC.
USA CANADA ENGLAND

BibleLog Thru the New Testament Series
Book 1 **When God Left Footprints** (Matthew thru John)
Book 2 **Good News to Go** (Acts thru 1 Corinthians)
Book 3 **Priority Mail** (2 Corinthians thru Philemon)
Book 4 **Home At Last** (Hebrews thru Revelation)

BibleLog Thru the Old Testament Series
Book 1 **Let There Be Life** (Genesis thru Ruth)
Book 2 **Who's Running This Kingdom?** (1 Samuel thru 2 Chronicles)
Book 3 **Tales, Tunes, and Truths** (Ezra thru Song of Songs)
Book 4 **Watchmen Who Wouldn't Quit** (Isaiah thru Malachi)

BibleLog for Adults is an inductive Bible study series designed to take you through the Bible in 2 years if you study one session each week. This eight-book series correlates with SonPower's **BibleLog** series for youth. You may want to use **BibleLog** in your daily quiet time, completing a chapter a week by working through a few pages each day. Or you may want to use this series (along with the SonPower **BibleLog** series) in family devotions with your teenagers. This book also includes a leader's guide for use in small groups.

Scripture taken from the *Holy Bible, New International Version,* © 1973, 1978, 1984, International Bible Society. Used by permission of Zondervan Bible Publishers.

Library of Congress Catalog Card Number: 91-65460
ISBN: 0-89693-869-7

Recommended Dewey Decimal Classification: 227
Suggested Subject Heading: BIBLE STUDY: EPISTLES

C O N T E N T S

BEFORE YOU BEGIN

Welcome to Book 1 in the
BibleLog Thru the New Testament Series

Though the Bible continues to be one of the world's best-selling books, few people are familiar enough with it to comprehend "the big picture." They may know many of the specific stories about Abraham, Samson, Jonah, Jesus, Peter, Paul, and so forth. Yet most people are unsure how these characters fit into the broad historic groupings—patriarchs, judges, kings, prophets, Gospels, epistles, etc.

That's why we are introducing the **BibleLog Thru the New Testament Series.** The purpose of the **BibleLog** studies is to guide you through the New Testament in one year, at the rate of one session per week. This series eliminates the perceived drudgery of Bible reading by removing unnecessary references and explaining the material in clear terms that anyone can understand. The pace should be fast enough to propel you through the material without getting bogged down, yet slow enough to allow you to see things you never noticed before. First-time readers will feel completely at ease as they explore the Bible on their own. Yet no matter how many times a person has been through the Bible, this study will provide fresh insight.

WHAT MAKES BIBLELOG DIFFERENT?

Countless thousands of adults have, at some point in their lives, decided to read through the Bible. Pastors, Sunday School teachers, Bible study leaders, or peers have preached the benefits of "Read your Bible," "Get into the Word," "Meditate on Scripture," and so forth. And after hearing so many worthwhile challenges, a lot of determined, committed adults have dusted off the covers of their Bibles and set themselves to the task ahead.

They usually make a noble effort too. The first couple of Bible books whiz past before they know it. The next few books aren't quite as fast-paced, but they have their strong points. Then comes a tough passage. In most cases, the Gospels are enough to do in even the most eager readers. And instead of feeling like they've accomplished something, all that those people feel is guilt because they didn't finish what they started.

That's why this Bible study series was developed. It calls for a one-year commitment on your part to get through the New Testament. By following the session plans provided, you only need to complete one session each week to accomplish your one-year goal. You won't read the entire New Testament word-for-word, but you will go much more in-depth than most of the New Testament overviews you may have tried. You will still be challenged just to get through the major flow of New Testament action in one year.

WHAT ARE THE FEATURES OF BIBLELOG?

❏ **THE WHOLE BIBLE** Not a verse-by-verse study, but an approach that hits all the books without skipping major passages.

❏ **THE RIGHT PACE** By completing one session each week (a couple of pages per day), you will get through the New Testament in one year.

❏ **A FRESH APPROACH** The inductive design allows you to personally interact with biblical truth. Longer, drier passages are summarized in the text, and difficult passages are explained, but you are kept involved in the discovery process at all times.

❏ **INSTANT APPLICATION** Each weekly session concludes with a **Journey Inward** section of practical application that allows you to respond to the content immediately. The goal is to help you apply the truths of the Bible today.

❏ **GROUP STUDY OPTION** A leader's guide is included to promote discussion and further application, if desired. After a week of self-study, a time of group interaction can be very effective in reinforcing God's truth. Each book covers 13 weeks.

❏ **REASONABLE PRICE** The entire set of 4 New Testament **BibleLog** books costs no more than a basic Bible commentary. And after completing the series, you will have a self-written commentary of the New Testament for future reference.

❏ **48 DIFFERENT TOPICS** Over a one-year period of study, you will be challenged to apply what the Bible has to say about 48 different topics, including your relationship with Jesus, rejection, integrity, commitment, self-image, empathy, eternity, and much more.

HOW CAN YOU GET THE MOST OUT OF BIBLELOG?

We recommend a group study for this series, if possible. If group members work through the content of the sessions individually during the week, the time your group needs to spend going over facts will be greatly reduced. With the content portion completed prior to the group meeting, your group time can emphasize the application of the biblical concepts to your individual members. A leader's guide is included at the back of the book to direct you in a review of the content. But the real strength of the leader's guide is to show you how to apply what you are learning. If you don't have the opportunity to go through this series with a group, that's OK too. Just be sure to think through all the **Journey Inward** sections at the end of each session.

FROM THE AUTHORS

Don't you just love to get mail? Not that junky stuff that says you have won either $20 billion or a free toaster if you attend an all-expenses-paid time-sharing demonstration for a condo in Boise. But rather personal, handwritten mail with key words underlined three times and hearts instead of dots over the *i*'s.

When you're away from home and feeling lonely and homesick, nothing in the world looks as good as a letter from home. When a close friend is on a long vacation, a letter or postcard from that person can ease your empty feelings till he or she gets back home.

Yes, mail can be a tremendous boost to us. And, depending on who it's from, some mail is more of a boost than others. Much of the New Testament is a collection of letters written by the Apostle Paul, and there's not a piece of junk mail among them. This book will take you through 11 of Paul's letters. (If you just completed Book 2 of this series, you've already read two: Romans and 1 Corinthians.)

In some ways, Paul's letters are much like ones you might write. They contain personal greetings, heartfelt emotions, encouraging words, and challenges for his readers to keep going in spite of any opposition they face. But Paul's letters have one major distinction. They were written by the inspiration of God. So as you read through them, don't read casually.

Paul's letters apply to Christians today just as much as they did for the Christians of the first century. You'll find everything you look for in a letter—advice for improving relationships, comfort regarding the things that get you down, hope for a future that's better than the present, suggestions for ways to handle criticism, and the opportunity to get to know the writer a lot better. By the time you get through this book, you should know Paul almost as well as you know your other friends. And if you pay attention to what he writes, he will help you know *yourself* a lot better as well.

Pam & Stan Campbell

*Vulnerability means letting
others see who we really are.*

CAN YOU SEE
THE REAL ME?

(2 Corinthians 1–4)

R ead through the following situations and describe how you would respond in each instance.

SITUATION #1—You've always wanted to be involved in community theater, though you haven't had drama experience or speech classes. Every time you hear of tryouts, you almost go out for a part. But this time the play is *Camelot*—probably your all-time favorite. You just *know* that you are the person for the leading role, so you memorize the lines for an audition. You do a good job, and the director seems impressed. You wait expectantly for the results. But when she calls, she explains that the leading roles have been assigned to "more experienced" actors. She offers you one of the minor roles and gives you a couple of days to think about it. You didn't want your family to know about your audition until you could hit them with the big news of your starring role. But the next day your son asks, "How did the tryouts go for *Camelot*?" How would you respond?

SITUATION #2—In the past couple of days, nothing has seemed to go right. Your children are fighting a lot. A good friend is suddenly beginning to talk a lot about death and the unknown, and you're worried about him. You made a major mistake in the research report that you really needed to finish and turn in last week. Your dog ran away, which isn't unusual. But he didn't come home last night, which is strange for him. Your husband/wife seems distant lately, acting as if you are no longer important to him/her. And on top of everything else, you've been feeling really insecure—scared of the future, and you don't know why. You figure your Bible study group will get you pepped up again, but your leader is on vacation. The substitute group leader says, "Tonight I think we should really open up and share the things that are bothering us. Don't hold anything back." Then he looks right into your eyes and says, "Let's start with you." How much would you share with this stranger and your fellow small group members?

SITUATION #3 — There's a young woman at work who seems to be a real loner. But for the past several months you've been trying to talk to her, eat lunch with her occasionally, and be friendly. You've invited her to your Bible study group a couple of times, but she hasn't come. She never really says much to you, but you keep trying to be nice. One day she's talking to someone else at lunch. You go up, speak to her, and ask who her friend is. Her reply shocks you: "This is a *real* friend, not someone like you who doesn't really care about me. Why don't you go back to all your goody-goody church friends and leave us alone?" How do you respond to her?

We all find ourselves in positions where we don't know exactly what to say or how to act. We are accused of things we didn't do. People we trust betray us. Our hopes and dreams are shattered, and there's really no way for anyone else to know how we feel.

Most of the time we'd just as soon stick our heads in the sand and retreat from the human race. But giving up is never the answer. When the world seems to be falling apart around you, it needs your strong example more than ever. And in this session, you should find some help to stand firm even when you don't feel like standing at all.

 JOURNEY ONWARD

This session will pick up your biblical journey with Paul's follow-up letter to the church in Corinth (the Book of 2 Corinthians). If you recently completed Book 2 of the **BibleLog Thru-the-New-Testament** Series, you should recall from 1 Corinthians several of the "qualities" of the Christians in Corinth. They were immature. They were sinful (and often proud of it). Their worship habits were atrocious. They bickered over which apostle was the best. And when Paul had previously visited Corinth, he said he had to give them "milk" because they weren't at all ready for the "meat" of Christianity (1 Corinthians 3:2). After Paul's visit (which lasted a year and a half [Acts 18:7-11]), he had written them to deal with these problems.

Now, less than a year later, Paul felt the need to write another letter to the Corinthians. As you will see, they were still having problems. But this time, Paul discovered that *he* was right in the middle of some of their conflicts— even though he had done nothing to deserve the hostility that some people were directing toward him. As you read 2 Corinthians, note how personal this letter is. Paul is very open about himself and his feelings.

Read 2 Corinthians 1:1-11.
Who was with Paul when he wrote 2 Corinthians? (2 Corinthians 1:1-2)

As he opened his letter with praise to God, what three titles did Paul use for God? What does each title tell you about God? (1:3-4)

Why are we allowed to experience unpleasant situations? (1:4-7)

Getting Personal—*What is the most recent unpleasant situation that you have experienced? How did you make it through this situation?*

(NOTE: Paul is using "we," "our," and "us" throughout this book. He was actually referring only to himself in most cases, but as he talked about himself he chose not to use "I" and "me.")

How unpleasant had Paul's hardships become? (1:8-9)

How did Paul make it through his difficult circumstances? (1:9-11)

Conflict in Corinth

As you go through 2 Corinthians, you will find several instances where Paul referred to accusations made against him. It seems that several teachers of false doctrines were doing all they could to discredit Paul's authority. As Paul wrote, he continued to justify his work and his call as an apostle. He also refuted the untruths of his accusers.

Read 2 Corinthians 1:12-24.
What was Paul's boast to the Corinthians? (1:12-14)

What was Paul's original plan in regard to the Corinthians? (1:15-16)

But Paul had changed his plans. Why? (1:23–2:2)

Apparently this was one of the issues raised by the troublemakers in Corinth. They were telling the people something to the effect of, "See. Paul can't be trusted. He says one thing, and then turns around and does another. So how can you believe anything the guy says?" This accusation was the source of Paul's "boast" that he had never distorted the Gospel. And it led to a long defense of his actions (1:12-24 and throughout the entire Book of 2 Corinthians). Yes, he *had* changed his plans to visit Corinth, but he had done it to spare their feelings. It seems that Paul had made a short, unscheduled stop previously, which had caused the Corinthians some grief (1:23–2:1). It was to avoid further pain that Paul canceled his plans to return again. Yet he wanted the individuals in the church to continue to persevere. What had God done that would help them to do so? (1:21-22)

Getting Personal—*Have you ever been accused of saying one thing and doing another? Were you guilty? How did the accusation make you feel?*

Read 2 Corinthians 2:1-17.
Instead of a personal visit back to Corinth, Paul wrote them again. (This letter was probably written between the letters of 1 Corinthians and 2 Corinthians, and was not meant by God to be part of the Scripture.) Paul still hoped to get back to Corinth eventually (2 Corinthians 13:1). In the meantime, he didn't want to do anything that would damage his relationship with the Corinthians. How did Paul feel when he wrote the middle letter? Why? (2:2-4)

It seems that Paul wasn't the only person who had encountered some conflict with the Corinthian church members. Another unnamed man had done something that the church people thought deserved discipline. The Corinthians had apparently come a long way from the time when they looked the other way while one of their members continued to sleep with his father's wife (1 Corinthians 5:1-2). But in this case, Paul wanted to make sure they didn't get *too* carried away with their role as disciplinarians. What advice did Paul give them? (2 Corinthians 2:5-9)

Perhaps this man's offense had been against Paul. Or perhaps the church members were trying to impress Paul with their "watchfulness" instead of really caring about the man who had been disciplined. Why did Paul say they should forgive the man? (2:10-11)

In outlining his travel schedule to the Corinthians, Paul explained that he had quickly moved on from Troas to Macedonia. Why? (2:12-13)

(NOTE: Remember the person named here. He turns up from time to time throughout Paul's letters. And in Session 12, you'll examine an entire letter from Paul to this person.)

Paul knew that wherever he went he could search for an audience willing to hear his message. Why did Paul offer thanks at this point? (2:14)

Maybe certain smells have special significance to you. An evergreen might automatically bring wonderful thoughts of past Christmases. A sniff of the first yard mowed in the spring can spark the anticipation of freshness and freedom. And to the ancient Romans, certain smells reminded them of victory. When they had a big victory parade, they burned spices and incense while the soldiers marched and the people cheered. Paul painted a similar picture of Christianity—complete with the smells. When the "aroma" of Christians is sensed by God, He is reminded of Christ, and is pleased.

When an animal was sacrificed to God in the Old Testament, it was said to have been "a pleasing aroma" to the Lord. (See Exodus 29:18, for example.) And it makes sense that Christians as "living sacrifices" (Romans 12:1) would be symbolically sweet-smelling. But not everyone enjoys the pleasant fragrance of Christianity. Why don't some people appreciate it? (2 Corinthians 2:15-16)

Getting Personal—*Do others think you emit "a pleasing aroma" of Christ? Why or why not?*

What made Paul distinctive when compared to many of the other preachers of his time? (2:17)

A New Covenant
Read 2 Corinthians 3:1-18.

The problem with teachers of false doctrine had gotten so bad that many churches were requiring letters of recommendation from prospective ministers. As Paul wrote, he was a little reluctant to pat himself on the back. And he didn't think he needed a letter of recommendation after everything he had already done for the churches. So he said something to the effect of, "You want a letter of recommendation? I'll *give* you a letter of recommendation!" What did Paul submit as his letter of recommendation? (3:1-3)

Paul said that competence as a minister is something supplied by God. God's ministers have a New Covenant to proclaim. The emphasis is no longer on the letter of the Law, which had served its purpose in pointing out human sinfulness. The focus is now on the Holy Spirit (3:4-6). How does the New Covenant compare with the old one? (3:6-11)

Paul reminds his readers about the story of Moses as he came down from Mount Sinai after talking to God (Exodus 34:29-35). His face radiated God's glory so much that he had to wear a veil before the people would come close enough to talk to him. But Moses' radiance (from the Old Covenant) faded away eventually. The glory of our New Covenant with God has a nonfading radiance. How has the New Covenant affected our relationship with God? (2 Corinthians 3:12)

But some of the Jewish people were still behind a type of "veil" that prevented them from understanding that their Law was a foreshadowing of the coming of Jesus. How can the veil be removed? (3:13-17)

What becomes possible after the veil is removed? (3:18)

Getting Personal—*Are you being transformed into Christ's likeness?*

Read 2 Corinthians 4:1-7.
How did Paul describe his style of ministry? (4:1-2)

After doing everything he could to legitimately proclaim the Gospel, Paul realized that even then he wouldn't be able to convince everyone who heard him. Why not? (4:3-6)

The Gospel (the truth about Jesus) is a genuine treasure. And you expect to find treasure in a safe, secure place of honor. But God chooses to entrust imperfect, often weak, people with the Gospel. What image did Paul use to describe that fact? (4:7)

Getting Personal—*How well do these verses in 2 Corinthians 4 describe your ministry to others?*

Confidence in Conflict
Read 2 Corinthians 4:8-18.
Christians can be "hard pressed," "perplexed," "persecuted," and "struck down." But even while these nasty things are happening, of what can they be confident? (4:8-9)

Why do you think Paul didn't just give up the struggle to spread the truth of Christianity after he encountered so much opposition? (4:10-15)

Getting Personal — *How do you respond when you are persecuted, tired, or feeling defeated?*

Even though we may be outwardly persecuted or tired or seemingly defeated, how can we continue to persevere? (4:16)

Whenever you are going through a particularly hard time, what should you always keep in mind? (4:17-18)

Unfortunately, not many of us have learned to adopt Paul's perspective. When people cause us problems, we usually don't reveal our true emotions. Sometimes we keep our feelings to ourselves. Sometimes we gossip about whoever it is who is bothering us. Sometimes we yell, kick, and scream. And many times our responses make the problem worse instead of better.

 JOURNEY INWARD

If you had been the Apostle Paul, how would you have handled the situation in Corinth? Don't forget that he had previously spent 1 1/2 years with these people. He had followed up his visit with the letter we know as 1 Corinthians. He had returned to Corinth for what he recalled as a "painful visit." But in spite of all he had done, the church continued to have major problems. At the top of the problem list were a group of deceivers passing themselves off as preachers and trying to convince the Corinthian church that *Paul* was the one not to be trusted.

By this time, would you have reached the giving-up point? Or would you have told the Corinthians (in no uncertain terms) exactly what you thought about their immature church and their phony "religious" leaders? Paul did neither. Rather, he poured his heart out to those people and in doing so gave us a valuable lesson in **vulnerability.**

After all Paul had been through, it wasn't fair that he would need to defend himself to a group of people who were nowhere near his level of spiritual maturity. But he did, and he did so willingly. And if Paul could do it, then most of us should surely be willing to be open with others.

To determine how vulnerable you are, fill in the following grid. A number of situations are listed down the left side and a selection of people are across the top. Put an X mark in the boxes that indicate those with whom you would *willingly* share each bit of information. Put an O in the boxes that indicate the people you would *reluctantly* share that information with. Leave blank the people you wouldn't tell under any circumstances. Mark all the boxes that apply. (You may need to use your imagination for some of the people listed.)

	Spouse	Children	Parents	Boss	Church Friends	Brother/Sister(s)	Best Friend(s)	Small Group	Sunday School Teacher	Pastor	God	Counselor/Psychologist	Casual Acquaintance	Coworker
Your spouse forgot your birthday, and it really hurts.														
You think your boss made a pass at you.														
You would like a favor from this person.														
You just received a raise.														

	Spouse	Children	Parents	Boss	Church Friends	Brother/Sister(s)	Best Friend(s)	Small Group	Sunday School Teacher	Pastor	God	Counselor/Psychologist	Casual Acquaintance	Coworker
You just got fired.														
You have severe doubts about Christianity.														
You are really tempted to get involved an extramarital relationship.														
You're really mad at this person.														
You think you should change careers.														
You wonder if and when you should have children.														
Your child is failing in school.														
God has answered a prayer you've been praying for months.														
Your teenager is responsible for a child out of wedlock.														
You're kind of thinking about suicide.														
Your spouse just asked for a divorce.														
You're being intimidated by a co-worker.														

A large percentage of Xs and Os in your grid indicate a high level of vulnerability. Of course, you don't want to tell *everybody* you see *everything* you're feeling. (People will begin to dive for cover when they see you coming.) But neither should you stuff your doubts, fears, frustrations, hurts, and disappointments. You need to feel free to share intimate thoughts with people who really care for you.

If you're not a naturally vulnerable person, you should start slowly. Select one person at first whom you can really trust. See if that person will be willing to talk with you. Then share one or two things about yourself that aren't too terribly earthshaking. (Don't dump everything at once!) Over time, you can gradually develop the relationship until you can open up to that person more completely. You should also find that you are able to talk more freely with other people as well.

And don't just share your problems. Nobody enjoys the company of a constant whiner. If you appreciate someone's good qualities, don't be afraid to say so. If you need someone's help, remember that the worst thing he or she can do is say no. Don't be so hesitant to ask. And be vulnerable enough to offer *your* help whenever you see the opportunity.

Paul knew that it is through our vulnerability that others are able to see the God whom we serve. So pick out a person or two this week and start to open up. You stand to gain a number of invaluable opportunities and life-long relationships. And all you have to lose are some invisible walls that probably need to come down anyway.

 KEY VERSE:
"Thanks be to God, who always leads us in triumphal procession in Christ and through us spreads everywhere the fragrance of the knowledge of Him" (2 Corinthians 2:14).

There's more than money involved in the matter of giving.

2

GIVING TILL IT
HURTS NO MORE

(2 Corinthians 5–9)

The official-looking letter addressed to you from the law firm of Northam, Southern, Easton, Westin, and Fred contained good news and bad news. First the bad news: your great-aunt Lulu is dead. But since you had never met Aunt Lulu, the news of her death truthfully didn't affect you all that much. Your mom hadn't even seen her in 22 years. When you asked why not, she just said, "Your great-aunt was a little eccentr . . . , interes. . . . Dear, your Aunt Lulu was a nut case."

You were sorry she had died, of course, but the good news was even more shocking—you had been named in her will! According to the letter, you were supposed to show up at her lawyer's office in two weeks.

Fourteen days never went by more slowly. Your anticipation got to the point where you couldn't concentrate on anything during the day and couldn't sleep during the night. Mom called and did her best to try to keep you down to earth.

"Congratulations, dear. You can only hope that you'll get her complete collection of ceramic Civil War generals' wives. Or the ball of string that she's been collecting since 1933."

But nothing could contain your excitement. The big day finally arrived, and you put on your best suit. (If you were going to be rich, why not dress like it?) To be honest, you weren't expecting all that much from somebody you never met, but you could hope, couldn't you?

You met in Mr. Southern's plush office, and he handed out pens and paper to everyone present (legal pads, of course). Then he began to read.

"I, Mrs. Lulu McKenzie, being of sound mind and body, am richer than anyone can possibly imagine. And I am leaving my entire fortune to my cats, with the exception of a few token gifts to the friends and relatives who least offended me during my lifetime. I leave to them," the lawyer paused and swallowed hard, "anything they want, and as much as they want. The only stipulations are that they have to ask for specific things, and they may only take 60 seconds to compile their lists. Requests for large amounts of cash are unoriginal and will not be considered. But any other requests that are made will be honored. My cats get the rest."

Mr. Southern clicked a stopwatch in his hand and said, "You have one minute. Go!"

Time yourself for 60 seconds and write your requests below.

How did you do with your list? Did you write furiously for the entire 60 seconds, or did you run out of ideas before your time was up?

Here's a more important question. How many of the things on your list were for people other than yourself? (And it's no fair saying, "They can ride in my new Porsche.") How many things were exclusively for someone other than yourself?

An opportunity like the one above would have been a wonderful time to consider known, specific needs of other people and make a request on their behalf. Perhaps you did. But most often our thoughts are primarily on ourselves rather than the needs of others.

JOURNEY ONWARD

The focus of this session is going to be on giving. As you work your way through this section of 2 Corinthians, look for two things. First, look for things that Paul mentions as God's gifts to us. Second, look for ways that you can become a more effective giver. (HINT: There are more ways to give than shelling out your money.)

If you remember where we left off in the last session, Paul was describing how we as Christians have the treasure of the Gospel, but it is contained in our bodies, which are symbolized by "jars of clay." And he went on to describe the wear and tear that our bodies go through. This session begins with some terrific promises in regard to our bodies.

Read 2 Corinthians 5:1-21.

Think of your body as a place to live—a type of dwelling place. Using that illustration, how does your earthly body compare to the heavenly body you will eventually receive? (2 Corinthians 5:1)

We are promised better things in the future. But how can we be sure that what we have been promised will actually come to pass? (5:2-5)

If you've ever done much camping out, you may be very glad that you don't have to live in a tent all the time. Tents are temporary housing, and after a long camping trip you're usually more than happy to get back to your own bed, your own shower, your own stove and refrigerator, and so forth. Paul makes the same observation in regard to our earthly bodies. They do OK for a while, but it's a tremendous comfort to be able to look forward to something better. But while we're in possession of our earthly bodies, what must we remember to do? (5:6-9)

Why should we take care to put our earthly, temporary bodies to good use? (5:10)

What is a natural result of a healthy fear of (respect for) God? (5:11)

Getting Personal— *Do you fear God? In what way?*

Perhaps some of Paul's critics had accused him of being a littly loopy. Or maybe he was reminded of some of his bold actions in spreading the Gospel that may have seemed "insane" to onlookers. But Paul was able to say that whether or not he was out of his mind, he remained motivated. What things kept Paul going? (5:12-13)

(NOTE: Don't forget that Paul uses pronouns like "us" and "we" to refer to himself.)
What key truth did Paul steadfastly cling to? (5:14-15)

How much difference does belief in Jesus make in a person's life? (5:16-17)

What is our responsibility as believers in Jesus? (5:18-21, esp. v. 20)

Read 2 Corinthians 6:1-2.
What is special about this time of history—after Jesus' first coming to earth and before His second coming? (6:1-2)

Paul the Persecuted
Read 2 Corinthians 6:3-18.
Paul reminded the church at Corinth that he had done nothing to cause anyone to "stumble" over the Gospel or to doubt the sincerity of his ministry. Then he listed a number of things he had experienced as a servant of God. Some are good experiences and others are negative. Read through his list in 2 Corinthians 6:3-10, and list everything that also applies to *your* experience as a Christian.

Reminding the Corinthians that he is still being vulnerable with them, Paul asks them to do the same for him (6:11-13). Again, the attitudes of the people in Corinth were probably being influenced by the presence of false teachers there. What strong advice did Paul give them, and why did he advise them the way he did? (6:14-18)

Read 2 Corinthians 7:1-16.
Why should Christians keep striving for perfection? (7:1)

After his strong instructions to the Corinthians, Paul devoted a section of his letter to telling them the things they were doing right. To begin with, he again affirmed his own innocence and sincerity (to answer any accusers). And after he made sure they knew he was being totally honest, what did he want them to know? (7:2-4)

How had Paul been cheered up by the Corinthians when he was really depressed—even though the Corinthians probably didn't know anything about it? (7:5-7)

Getting Personal—*Who cheers you up when you are depressed?*

Paul again recalled his previous letter to the church in Corinth that had caused them pain. But he told them he wasn't sorry he had written it. Why not? (7:8-9)

What is the significant difference between godly sorrow and worldly (self-centered) sorrow? (7:10)

What were the results of the Corinthians' godly sorrow? (7:11)

So Paul was cheered by the response of the Corinthians. The entire church benefited from the experience. And even people who heard about the turn-around of the Corinthians were thrilled. Who was one such person? (7:12-16)

Money Matters

So far the Book of 2 Corinthians has primarily focused on Paul's defense of his actions and apostleship. He didn't want the church at Corinth to have a single doubt about his motives or attitudes. Having completed a lengthy section of personal defense, he next turned his attention to church business.

Read 2 Corinthians 8:1-24.
After encouraging the Corinthians for the things they were doing right, Paul praised the church in Macedonia. What had the Macedonian church done that was so noteworthy? (8:1-4)

How were the Macedonian church members able to do what they did? (8:5)

Getting Personal — *Do you consider yourself a generous person? Why or why not? What specific things prevent you from being generous?*

Paul urged the Corinthians to follow the example of the Macedonians. He told the Corinthians that they were already excelling in many areas — including faith, speech, knowledge, earnestness, and love. Why did he think this one other area was so important? (8:6-8)

How had Jesus previously set an example in this area? (8:9)

The church in Corinth had a good history of giving, but Paul didn't want them to rest on the laurels of what they had done last year (8:10). What more did he want them to do? (8:11)

What is more important than the size of a gift? (8:12)

What should happen among Christian churches if they give properly? (8:13-15)

The money being collected was to be used for the poverty-stricken Christians in Jerusalem (1 Corinthians 16:1-4). Paul was sending Titus and two other men to oversee the collection of the gift from the Corinthian church (2 Corinthians 8:17-18, 22). What did Paul want to be very careful about? (8:20-21)

Getting Personal—*Can you be trusted to handle the collection of money? Are there any precautions you need to take to prevent criticism or suspicion?*

Read 2 Corinthians 9:1-15.
After Paul's big challenge to the Corinthian church, he paused to say that he knew the Corinthians were eager to help (9:1-5). In fact, after praising the Macedonians to the Corinthians, he said he had been bragging about the Corinthians to the Macedonians. (Paul was justifiably proud of everyone who was contributing to the needs of the church and the spread of the Gospel.) He just wanted the Corinthians to be prepared if anybody from Macedonia happened to tag along when Titus went to Corinth. (No matter how clean you keep the house, you like to know if company's coming.)

What same basic rule applies to both giving and gardening? (9:6)

What are three possible attitudes you can have concerning giving? (9:7)

What kind of giver is God? (9:8-9)

What opportunities do people have who have been blessed by God with material possessions? (9:10-11)

A cheerful and generous gift can have many positive effects of which the giver may not even be aware. Review 2 Corinthians 9:12-14 and list all the things Paul said would happen as a result of the Corinthians' gift.

As Paul concluded this section on giving and gifts, he just couldn't "wrap up" the subject without reminding us of God's greatest gift to us — His Son, Jesus. What word did Paul use to describe God's gift, and why do you think he chose that word? (9:15)

After Paul went through all the personal and spiritual benefits of cheerful giving, he suggested the question that some skeptics may have been thinking: "What did God ever do for me?" Paul didn't come right out and say, "Well, let's see. Besides an abundance of daily blessings there was also the gift of His only begotten Son who left heaven to come to earth so He could suffer, bleed, die a horrible death, and then come back to life in order for us to call God our Father, live forever, and not have to worry about going to hell. Aside from that, not much." No, Paul was classier than that. But he did suggest that we all think about the "indescribable" gift of Jesus Christ. It's good advice.

 JOURNEY INWARD

Before we go any farther, be warned that it's not appropriate for you to try to overlook this session by saying: "I don't have money to give. I'm living on a small salary and trying to make ends meet. So this stuff doesn't really apply to me."

No one wants to dispute your financial situation. Maybe you are pinching your pennies so tightly that your thumbs look like tiny impressions of Abraham Lincoln. But there's much more than mere money involved in this crucial matter of **giving.**

To begin with, we must remember that God is a giver. We've just considered the gift of His Son. But Paul also reminded the Corinthians that God had given them earthly bodies. And when those bodies wear out, He provides heavenly, eternal bodies (5:1). We have the gift of the Holy Spirit (5:5). We are given an entirely fresh and new outlook on life (5:17). We have spiritual bonds to other people who care about us (9:14). And Paul could have gone on. In the space below, list some of the gifts of God for which you are grateful.

We need to also remember that there are many ways to "give" without reaching into your wallet or purse. And there are several attitudes you can have while you're giving (9:7). For each of the methods of giving listed below, check the appropriate box that indicates your attitude.

	Nongiver	Reluctant Giver	Sense-of-duty Giver	Cheerful Giver
Nonmonetary gifts (time, energies, etc.) to other Christians (8:5)				
Nonmonetary gifts to God (8:5)				
Sharing the gift of the Gospel (5:18-20)				
Gifts of money/possessions to other needy Christians (8:7)				
Monetary gifts to your church (9:7)				
Giving when it really hurts to give (8:2)				
Other types of giving: _____				

Paul told the Corinthians to finish what they had started (8:10-12). Perhaps they had done well for a while in collecting for the people in Jerusalem but had allowed their giving to taper off. It's easy to find other uses for our money, and we need to remember that there are almost always people around us who can use our help. Can you think of anyone in your church, business, or neighborhood who could use a little financial support right now? If so, list the name(s) below.

Remember that God isn't impressed by the size of our gifts. "If the willingness is there, the gift is acceptable according to what one has, not according to what he does not have" (8:12). The opening exercise of this session may have given you some insight into your level of willingness to give.

Once you begin to give back to God a certain percentage of what you make, the process becomes more natural with time. But don't make the mistake of thinking that giving will become a lot easier when you're making more money. If you don't develop a giving attitude when you're living on minimum wage, you aren't likely to have one no matter how much you eventually make. So begin this week to work on both the *practice* of giving and the *attitude* of giving. The rest of the world talks about "giving till it hurts." As Christians, we have the opportunity to "give till it feels great." (You may not exactly be a "cheerful" giver at first, but you will be in time as you see how God uses you to reach people for Him.)

 KEY VERSE:

"Remember this: Whoever sows sparingly will also reap sparingly, and whoever sows generously will also reap generously. Each man should give what he has decided in his heart to give, not reluctantly or under compulsion, for God loves a cheerful giver" (2 Corinthians 9:6-7).

*What kind of reflection of yourself would
you like to see in the mirror?*

3

THORNS AND ALL

(2 Corinthians 10-13)

Go stand in front of your bathroom mirror. Every morning you bounce joyfully out of bed and spring to this mirror to see how wonderful you look. (OK then. Every morning you drag your feeble body out of bed, feel your way to the bathroom, and slowly open your eyes to look at the creature that is staring back at you.) And even though you fix yourself up the best you can, you may still not be completely happy with the results. As you look at the mirror, take a complete inventory of yourself. Describe your reflection, noting any of those little imperfections that drive you crazy.

Blink your eyes and look at the mirror again. Imagine that the mirror now reflects the image of yourself that you *want* to see. It can be as truthful or as flattering as you would like. Describe the reflection of yourself that you would see in that mirror.

Now compare your two images. Are they exactly alike? Given the opportunity, most people would probably make a change or two between the way they actually are and the way they would like to be. Some people would probably make so many changes that nobody would recognize them any more.

You may have heard the true story about the time that the 17th-century British statesman, Oliver Cromwell, was having his portrait painted. Since this was before the days of Polaroids or 35-millimeter film, this portrait would determine the way Cromwell would be remembered by future generations. And as he sat down to have his image put on canvas, this is what he told the artist: "Mr. Lely, I desire you would use all your skill to paint my picture truly like me, and not flatter me at all; but remark all these roughnesses, pimples, warts, and everything as you see me, otherwise I will never pay a farthing for it" (*Anecdotes of Painting in England,* Horace Walpole).

There are a few—a very few—people in this world who can look at themselves and truly like what they see. That doesn't mean they think they are perfect. They see imperfections. They recognize that other people may be thinner, prettier, wealthier, and more muscular. Others may have whiter teeth, darker tans, and better hair. But a tremendous satisfaction comes with the realization that those other people aren't *you*, and that you have strengths, abilities, and a one-of-a-kind personality and character that no one else could ever duplicate.

 JOURNEY ONWARD

Paul was one such person. You'll remember from the last couple of sessions that he had been forced to defend himself to the Corinthian church because of some religious impostors who were trying to discredit him. As we'll see in this session, he finishes with a strong appeal for the Corinthians to take a close look at him—warts and all. This is one of the most intensely personal portions of the Bible. And Paul's model of honest, vulnerable appeal should be an example for us all.

Read 2 Corinthians 10:1-6.
How did Paul's letters to the Corinthians differ from his previous visits to see them? (2 Corinthians 10:1)

What warning did Paul give the Corinthians? (10:2)

Christians are involved in a type of warfare, and war is never pleasant. The words Paul uses to describe our role as Christians are strong ones—"fight," "demolish," "take captive," and "punish." Yet our battle is a spiritual one. What is it that we're supposed to demolish? (10:4-5)

What are we supposed to take captive? (10:5)

Getting Personal—*Do you have any particular thoughts that need to be taken captive?*

What are we supposed to punish? (10:6)

Paul's Defense
Read 2 Corinthians 10:7-18.
While Paul had previously fended off the accusations of troublemakers in Corinth, at this point he begins to confront them directly. What did he say was one of their problems? (10:7)

Paul felt his ministry was one of "building up" rather than "pulling down," but he was always ready to defend himself against accusers who said he was in error concerning his teaching about Jesus (10:8). The slanderers of Paul were probably classy and polished. They were no doubt smooth talkers to have infiltrated the Corinthian church so easily. So it would figure that they might attack Paul in regard to his communication skills. What was another of their complaints about Paul? (10:9-10)

How did Paul respond to this accusation? (10:11)

Paul wasn't trying to compete with these people on a personal level. His authority was from God, and he shouldn't have had to waste his time in constant defense of his ministry (though as you will soon see, he was able and willing to do so). How did Paul feel about this petty, jealous, competitive attitude? (10:12-14)

Getting Personal — *Step into Paul's shoes. How would you have responded to the jealous, competitive attitudes?*

Paul reminded the Corinthian church that he didn't need to boast to them. After all, he was the one who had taken them the Gospel in the first place. What did Paul hope to do as soon as the Corinthians had matured a little bit? (10:15-16)

How did the boasting of Paul's "competitors" affect him? (10:17-18)

Read 2 Corinthians 11:1-12.
Why did Paul ask the Corinthians to put up with a little of his "foolishness" so he could talk about himself? (11:1-3)

Then Paul suggested that the Corinthians shouldn't mind too much if he talked about himself. After all, he sarcastically noted, they didn't seem to care when the false teachers came into the church in Corinth and began to talk about a different Jesus, a different spirit, and a different gospel (11:4). And here's where Paul's healthy self-image was so important. He suggested that the Corinthians go ahead and compare him with the other "religious" folks in their church (whom he mockingly calls "super-apostles" [11:5]). Even though he may not have had the amount of training as a speaker that some of these other men had, how did Paul think he stacked up with them? (11:5-6)

Apparently Paul's critics had been trying to convince the Corinthians that, "You get what you pay for." It was a great scam; it suggested that Paul's no-charge messages had been worthless, and it gave them the opportunity to charge for their own services as "ministers." Paul responded by telling the Corinthians that, yes, he had "lowered" himself in order to "elevate" them, but what was the sin in that? Paul had received financial support from some churches, though he had never taken anything from the Corinthians. How did Paul feel about having churches support him? (11:7-9)

How did Paul plan to change his approach to administering the Gospel to those who needed to hear it? (11:10-12)

Super-Apostles
Read 2 Corinthians 11:13-33.
Paul finally came out and said what he truthfully felt about the "super-apostles" who had worked their way into the Corinthian church. How did he really feel about them? (11:13)

Why did he say these men acted the way they did? (11:14-15)

Paul affirmed that he was no fool (11:16). But, on the other hand, since the Corinthians seemed to be putting up with fools, he asked them to allow him to continue to do a little foolish "boasting" about himself (11:17-18). Paul's self-image was strong enough that he could stand and proclaim the truth when other people tried to put him down. Could the Corinthians make the same claim? Explain (11:19-21).

After noting how the false teachers had treated the Corinthians, Paul told the Corinthians to compare his credentials to theirs. Paul had the same rich Jewish background that the other guys had—as good Hebrews, descended from Abraham. But that was the past. Paul worked his way around to a current analysis of what was being done for the cause of Christ. And while Paul said he was "out of his mind" to speak of himself the way he was doing, he knew it was necessary. In the following space, list all the things Paul had suffered for the Gospel. Write small. His list of difficult circumstances may be a little longer than anyone else's you know (11:22-27).

After presenting the Corinthians with such an impressive list, Paul added, "Oh, yeah. I also feel pressure every day for the well-being of all the churches I've helped get started" (11:28). That thought should have hit the Corinthians where it hurt. Paul was beyond a doubt one of the busiest, most conscientious workers in the history of Christianity. And in allowing others to challenge his credibility, the Corinthians were only adding to his stress level.

Remember that Paul thought of the church as a unified body that functioned as a whole, whose joy or suffering could be affected by any single individual. What do you think he meant by his two questions in 2 Corinthians 11:29?

It seems that Paul just kept thinking of personal experiences to share with the Corinthian church. For example, there was his "Damascus incident." What had happened to him there? (11:30-33)

Read 2 Corinthians 12:1-6.

Of course, hard work alone does not make someone a good Christian or an effective leader (though Paul's work was always motivated by his love for Jesus). So Paul addressed the area of his personal relationship with Christ. What remarkable incident had Paul previously witnessed? (12:1-5)

Because Paul uses the third person here ("I know a man in Christ"), some believe that he was not talking about himself. But it seems to make sense that he was humbly referring to his own experience. Even though some of the specifics of this experience were forbidden to be shared with others, the very fact that Paul had waited 14 years to talk about this at all shows his level of humility.

Paul was quick to point out that telling the truth isn't boasting. Yet rather than being impressed with grandiose stories and visions, how did Paul want people to evaluate him? (12:6)

Thorny Problems
Read 2 Corinthians 12:7-21.

Why wasn't Paul concerned with becoming conceited about all he had done? (12:7)

No one knows exactly what this "thorn" was that Paul had to live with. Some have speculated that his problem may have been eye trouble, epilepsy, persistent opponents, migraine headaches, speech disability, or other things.

But we can't tell for sure. We *do* know that he would have liked to have gotten rid of it. He "pleaded" with God three times to have it taken away. But God didn't. Why not? (12:8-9)

What lesson did Paul learn from this experience? (12:10)

Getting Personal — *What is your "thorn in the flesh"? How have you learned from your experience with it?*

Paul kind of apologized for having to be so blunt with the Corinthians. He didn't really want to do it, but he knew the Christians in Corinth needed to see things more clearly. In summarizing what he thought about the so-called "super-apostles," Paul said something to the effect of: "I am nothing. But then, I'm in no way inferior to those guys" (12:11). If Paul was nothing, those impostors in Corinth had to have been less than nothing. And Paul wanted the Corinthian church members to discover that fact for themselves. What did he ask them to remember? (12:12-13)

Paul was planning a third trip to Corinth. What kind of relationship did he want to have with the people when he got there? (12:14-15)

Getting Personal — *Is there a particular person or ministry that God is leading you to?*

After joking about craftily "tricking" the Corinthians into receiving the Gospel by not charging them anything (12:16), Paul asked them to seriously consider his intentions before he got there again (12:17-19). Paul wanted everything to be all right by the time he got back to Corinth. Was he convinced that it would be? Explain (12:20-21).

Read 2 Corinthians 13:1-14.
Was Paul planning to be timid when he returned to Corinth? (13:1-4)

What request did Paul make of the Corinthians? (13:5-6)

Getting Personal — *Have you examined yourself to see whether you are in the faith? Why or why not?*

What did Paul promise to do for the Corinthians? (13:7-10)

In his final words as he signed off his letter, Paul once again challenged the Corinthian church members to be of one mind and live in peace (13:11-14). He knew that the troublemakers would still be in Corinth, and he could only pray that the Corinthians would act on the words in his letter.

Did the Corinthians respond to Paul's letter? If we piece together a few hints, we can get a pretty good indication of the answer. First, Paul had told the Corinthians that if they would shape up, he could expand his ministry in that area (10:15-16). Second, we know that Paul was planning to visit Corinth again (13:1). Third, Bible scholars tell us that there are strong indications that Paul wrote his letter to the Romans during this third visit to Corinth. And finally, as Paul wrote to the Romans he said, "Now . . . there is no more place for me to work in these regions" (Romans 15:23). So from all indications, it would seem that the Corinthians responded to Paul's pleas and restored the spiritual integrity of their church. (Don't you just love a happy ending?)

JOURNEY INWARD

Now the big question is: What effect will Paul's words to the Corinthians have on *your* life? More than likely, you're not allowing teachers of false doctrine to come into your church and interfere with the truth that is being taught there. You probably aren't gullible enough to let someone con you into thinking ridiculous things about God or His ministers. But let's bring it down to a more personal level. Do you ever allow other people to determine how you feel about *yourself*? This was certainly a potential problem for Paul. As those troublemakers attacked his personal abilities and reputation, what if Paul hadn't had his bold "back-in-your-face" attitude? Think what would have happened if Paul had caved in to their many cruel comments and left the Corinthians to fend for themselves. Paul's actions should inspire us to reconsider our levels of **self-image.**

In the space below, list the things that you like least about yourself. These can be things that you've observed on your own, or that other people have pointed out to you.

Keeping your list in mind, describe how these things affect each of the following areas of your life:

❑ The way you handle criticism

❑ Your relationships with other people

❑ The way you feel about God

❑ Your personality

Do you think the things that you don't like about yourself can be remedied? (Can you consciously work to eliminate some of them? Are some of them actually minor things that you are making a big deal about?) Go back and mark through everything on your list that you think is temporary.

Perhaps you still have a problem or two left. If so, perhaps these things are your "thorns," like Paul's thorn in the flesh. You can take care of any thorns in the same manner that Paul did—by realizing that God supplies enough grace (whether in the form of courage, patience, determination, or whatever) to help you live with those specific problems. If you allow God to see you through them, in what ways can your problems help make you strong? (12:10)

It is essential that you don't underestimate the importance of yourself or your ministry. We cannot let petty physical problems interfere with the important spiritual battles we are fighting. We must not turn our backs when we see non-Christians "masquerading" as servants of God. We can't afford to hang our heads in shame when accosted by others who try to use our weaknesses to dismiss the importance of Christianity.

True, it's hard to walk the fine line between humility and pride. But too much of what we call humility is actually cowardice.

Keep in mind that Paul's self-image was developed in the context of much suffering. But he never gave up. And he eventually got to the point where he could rejoice in his sufferings because they made him dependent on God, which made him stronger than ever.

With God's help, you can improve your self-image to where you can be proud of yourself—warts and all. But don't be surprised if, after a while, you're the only one who will see the warts. All anyone else will see is a strong, confident person who knows what life is all about.

 KEY VERSE:
"The weapons we fight with are not the weapons of the world. On the contrary, they have divine power to demolish strongholds. We demolish arguments and every pretension that sets itself up against the knowledge of God, and we take captive every thought to make it obedient to Christ" (2 Corinthians 10:4-5).

*Normally, people who have served time
in prison are more than happy to get out.*

4

FREEDOM COME,
FREEDOM GO

(Book of Galatians)

Lefty and Fletch huddled in a dark corner of their small, dank room. Their plans were almost complete. Before them sat everything they should need: grappling hooks, lockpicks, lots of rope, master keys, flashlights, and a floorplan of the prison.

"Better not let anyone see you with that stuff," said Fletch. "We don't want anything to spoil our plans now."

"That's for sure," replied Lefty. "But as soon as it gets dark, we go. Right?"

"Right!"

As soon as the sun dropped below the horizon, they were moving. Out through the door of their tiny, confining room. Down the corridor. A short run to the base of the prison wall. Lefty tossed up the grappling hook while Fletch watched for guards. Quickly up one side and down the other.

But suddenly sirens began to wail. Dogs started to bark. Guards ran toward them from all directions. And before they knew it, Lefty and Fletch found themselves staring down a number of rifle barrels and fanged throats. Soon they were standing before the warden. The warden scowled as he stared at them. "What am I gonna do with you two guys?" He asked. "I thought you promised that this would never happen again." Looking at his head guard, the warden asked, "This is the same problem we've been having, isn't it?"

"Yes, sir," the guard replied. "We caught them breaking into the prison again."

"Listen, guys," threatened the warden, "we just can't have any more of this. You two were paroled last month. You served your time, you behaved yourselves, and you were released. Now go out and enjoy your freedom!"

Lefty hung his head and dug a toe into the carpet. "We like it in here better, Warden. It's so much more secure than it is on the outside. That motel room we've been sharing is OK, but we miss all our friends. Can't we just stay for a little while?"

"No—not until visiting day," insisted the warden. Then he sent them away. But just as they were leaving the main gate, the head guard was almost sure he heard Lefty whisper to Fletch, "Next time we'll dig a tunnel!"

Fletch and Lefty are a little strange. Normally, people who have served their time in prison are more than happy to get out. Students who work and struggle through four years of college to earn a degree don't usually return the next fall to start as freshmen again. Very few 16-year-olds will study, practice, and take that nerve-racking test to get a driver's license, and then decide to never take the car out after that. In most cases when a kind of freedom has been earned or granted, we are anxious to begin to practice that freedom. But of course, there are exceptions to every rule.

 JOURNEY ONWARD

You will discover a drastic exception to that rule as you move on into the Book of Galatians in this session. The Galatian churches had a problem similar to the church in Corinth. (The Book of Galatians was written to a group of churches, though their exact location is debated.) You should recall that a number of false teachers had made their presence known in the Corinthian church and had challenged Paul's motives and authority as an apostle. In the Galatian churches, the dissenters were much more organized. They composed a group known as the Judaizers—Jews who had become Christians but who believed that Christians ought to adopt many of the Old Testament Jewish practices. (You'll see some of their specific opinions in this session.) Their loud vocal stand was causing the New Testament church (not just the Galatians) a lot of problems.

Read Galatians 1:1-24.

Paul's opening statement to the Galatian churches provides a good clue as to what one of the big problems might be. What would you suspect Paul would be leading up to? (Galatians 1:1-5, esp. v. 1)

Paul wasted no time delving right into the problems that he had heard about in Galatia. What was happening there, and how did Paul feel about it? (1:6-7)

How did Paul feel about people who distorted the truth of the Gospel? (1:8-10)

What made Paul such an authority on the subject, anyway? (1:11-12)

Why was Paul in such a good position to oppose the things the Judaizers were teaching? (1:13-14)

What had Paul experienced that changed his Jewish (Old Testament) way of thinking? (1:15-24)

After Paul's dramatic encounter with Jesus on the road to Damascus (Acts 9:1-19), he didn't immediately begin to preach. Most people believe Paul went to Arabia (Galatians 1:17) to be alone for a while to meditate and think through the recent events of his life. We know that it was three years before he began a ministry, and it is probably a safe assumption that during those three years God revealed to Paul a firsthand knowledge of Christian truth. This supposition fits with Paul's statement that, "I did not receive [the Gospel] from any man, nor was I taught it" (1:12).

Read Galatians 2:1-10.
When Paul began his ministry, it was under the supervision of the church in Jerusalem. And Paul quickly challenged their traditional way of thinking. While traveling with Barnabas, Paul had enlisted Titus to help them. Titus was a Christian, but he had been a Gentile convert instead of a Jewish one. Consequently, he had never been circumcised. (Every Jewish male baby was to have the foreskin of his penis cut off when he was eight days old [Genesis 17:12]. This was an outward sign that would separate him from the Gentiles, who at that time were heathen nations all around the Jews.) But Jesus had died for both Jews and Gentiles, leaving the first-century church with a big question: Is circumcision still required before a person can have a good standing with God? The Judaizers said yes. Paul said no. Titus was the test case before the church authorities in Jerusalem. What was their decision? (Galatians 2:1-5)

As the apostles in Jerusalem saw Paul in action, what did they realize about him? (2:6-10)

Peter vs. Paul
Read Galatians 2:11-20.
Even though the church council had made a decision on the circumcision issue, there was too much history, tradition, and strong opinion for the matter to be settled quickly and easily. Even Peter got lured into the trap of trying to keep the two groups separated, and Paul had to get on his case. What were the circumstances of the conflict? (2:11-13)

Since Peter was such a leader, lots of other people were following his example. The segregation was even practiced by Barnabas ("Mr. Encouragement," who was involved with Paul in his work with the Gentiles)! How did Paul deal with the situation? (2:14-16)

What is a Christian's relationship to the old law? (2:16-19)

To what degree should a Christian be committed to Jesus? Explain (2:20).

Law and Promise
Read Galatians 2:21.
Suppose that obedience to the Old Testament law could bring us to God. If we were able to obey all its laws, practice circumcision, and become righteous by doing so, what would that mean? (2:21)

Read Galatians 3:1-29.
Paul asks the Galatians a number of questions with obvious answers to get them to recall their initial conversion to Christianity (3:1-5). Then he referred to the example of Abraham. Even before the law was given by Moses, how was God able to declare Abraham righteous? (3:6)

How did Abraham's example apply to the Galatians (and to us)? (3:7-9)

After the law was given, how were we eventually able to get back to the arrangement that God had with Abraham? (3:10-14)

In summarizing what he had been saying (3:15-18), Paul stated that God made a promise to Abraham and his "seed" (meaning Jesus). About 430 years after that promise, the Law was given to Moses to pass on to the Israelites. But this Law by no means canceled the promise God had previously made. With Jesus, the promise of righteousness by faith again becomes valid. So was Paul saying the Old Testament Law wasn't really of any use? Explain (3:19-25).

With the limitations of the Law behind us, what is made available to us now? (3:26-27)

What distinctions should we be making within the church? (3:28-29)

Read Galatians 4:1-31.
Paul said to think of it this way: A young child may be heir to a huge fortune. But he won't get control of that fortune until he is old enough to oversee it properly. Until then, the estate will have guardians and trustees. Then, at an assigned age, the fortune will be turned over to the heir. Likewise, the Law was a "guardian" until, through Jesus, we could all become children of God entitled to all the rights and privileges He offers. Now we are the children and heirs of God (4:1-7).

Becoming a child of God is a tremendously freeing experience. The Law was restrictive and confining. In a sense, it was enslaving. Because many of the Galatians were Gentiles, they had never been under the Law. But they had been enslaved by another master—sin. Many had worshiped false gods and had practiced special ceremonies of their own. What were Paul's concerns as he addressed the Galatians? (4:8-20)

Again Paul returned to the example of Abraham. His first son, Ishmael, had been conceived—in the usual way—by Sarah's handmaid, Hagar. But his "real" son, Isaac, had been conceived in Sarah's previously barren womb as a direct result of God's promise. Hagar represented the Law, and she gave birth to a slave. Sarah, on the other hand, represented freedom, and she gave birth to "children of promise." Paul affirmed that we are the children of the free woman (4:21-31).

Read Galatians 5:1-21.

Though most of the Galatian people had never been under the Jewish law, they were being drawn to it by the Judaizers. What would be the consequences if the Galatians gave in to pressure to conform to the legalistic teachings of the Judaizers? (5:1-6)

Paul insisted that the Judaizers would eventually be punished for misleading the Galatians (and other churches). And he offered his own strong opinion about them. Some Bible translations interpret Paul's desire to be that the agitators would be "cut off" from the Galatians. Other versions are more direct. They record that Paul's suggestion was that since the Judaizers were so all-fired insistent that a little piece of foreskin be clipped off, why didn't they go ahead and "cut off" the whole thing! It's a bold statement, but then, Paul was a bold kind of guy (5:7-12)

When people try to live by the law, they encounter a lot of "don'ts." What things are listed as elements of the sinful nature that are to be avoided? (5:16-21)

Fruit of the Spirit
Read Galatians 5:22-26.
But when we allow the Spirit of God to control us rather than trying to follow the rigid structure of the law, God allows spiritual fruit to blossom in our lives. We begin to live by a set of "do's" rather than "don'ts." What characteristics reflect the work of the Holy Spirit? (5:22-26)

Getting Personal — *If you possessed the characteristics you've just listed (and acted on them), do you think you would need the law to tell you what is right and wrong? Do you think circumcision would matter one way or the other? Do you think any other way of life would be as effective?*

Read Galatians 6:1-18.
Of course, sin is still going to be around. And Paul wanted us to know how to deal with it. When we observe sin in someone else, how should we respond? (6:1-2)

How can we keep from falling into sin ourselves? (6:3-5)

At first reading, it might seem that verse 2 somewhat contradicts verse 5. But a clear difference is made in the original Greek language. When Paul tells us to "carry each other's burdens," the reference is to a heavy, crushing load. In the context, this probably refers to spiritual crises and temptations. The "load" we are instructed to carry in 6:5 refers to a soldier's backpack. We're never free to impose on others by handing off all our burdens. Rather, each person should carry his own burden (which Jesus has promised will be a light one [Matthew 11:28-30]) as well as pitching in to help others who may be struggling under an excessively heavy load.

Why is it so important to keep doing the right thing, even when we become tired of doing so? (Galatians 6:6-10)

While the Judaizers continued to boast about their outward mark of circumcision (even though they weren't able to obey the Law), what did Paul boast about? (6:11-18)

 JOURNEY INWARD

It's silly to think of people trying to break *into* jail. It's ridiculous to consider staying in college after you have your degree. It's ludicrous to think of a slave on a Roman galley ship being given his freedom and saying, "No thanks. I think I'll hang around here and row some more. The whippings, blisters, sweat, disease, and moldy meals aren't really all that bad."

Yet, on an even larger scale, the Galatian church members were just about to write off an even greater freedom—the freedom that Jesus provides from sin and spiritual bondage. They were about to choose instead the confining lifestyle of trying to live under the Old Testament Law. But Paul challenged them to reconsider. And his letter applies to us as well in regard to our **Christian freedom.**

We sometimes take the attitude that we should be avoiding temptation and eliminating sin from our lives. Fine. We should. But if that's as far as we go, we're still living under a legalistic system and not experiencing the freedom that could be ours. As we respond to the Holy Spirit and allow Him to have control of our lives, we should see the "fruit" that is mentioned in Galatians 5:22-23. When we become Spirit-controlled and fruitful, we can get to the point where we won't even have to be too concerned with the "don'ts." We'll be too busy "do"ing. And Christianity will take on a positive appeal rather than a negative tone.

So we should examine ourselves and see whether we're being controlled by our old, sinful natures or by the Holy Spirit. Below you will find Paul's list of acts of the sinful nature as well as a list of the fruit of the Spirit. After each characteristic listed, indicate how much your life reflects that specific trait (whether good or bad). Use a scale of 1 to 10, with 1 being "Never" and 10 representing "Always."

ACTS OF THE SINFUL NATURE NEVER   ALWAYS

Sexual Immorality	1	2	3	4	5	6	7	8	9	10
Impurity	1	2	3	4	5	6	7	8	9	10
Debauchery (indulgence in sensual pleasures)	1	2	3	4	5	6	7	8	9	10
Idolatry (putting other things before God)	1	2	3	4	5	6	7	8	9	10
Witchcraft	1	2	3	4	5	6	7	8	9	10
Hatred	1	2	3	4	5	6	7	8	9	10
Discord	1	2	3	4	5	6	7	8	9	10
Jealousy/Envy	1	2	3	4	5	6	7	8	9	10
Fits of Rage	1	2	3	4	5	6	7	8	9	10
Selfish Ambition	1	2	3	4	5	6	7	8	9	10
Dissensions (heavy quarreling)	1	2	3	4	5	6	7	8	9	10
Factions (selfish cliques)	1	2	3	4	5	6	7	8	9	10
Drunkenness	1	2	3	4	5	6	7	8	9	10
Orgies	1	2	3	4	5	6	7	8	9	10
Other (you name it)	1	2	3	4	5	6	7	8	9	10

FRUIT OF THE SPIRIT   NEVER   ALWAYS

Love	1	2	3	4	5	6	7	8	9	10
Joy	1	2	3	4	5	6	7	8	9	10

	NEVER							ALWAYS		
Peace	1	2	3	4	5	6	7	8	9	10
Patience	1	2	3	4	5	6	7	8	9	10
Kindness	1	2	3	4	5	6	7	8	9	10
Goodness	1	2	3	4	5	6	7	8	9	10
Faithfulness	1	2	3	4	5	6	7	8	9	10
Gentleness	1	2	3	4	5	6	7	8	9	10
Self-control	1	2	3	4	5	6	7	8	9	10

Here you have the opportunity to compare the "sinful" parts of your life with the "fruitful" ones. A good starting point might be to see if the total of your 9 responses under the Fruit of the Spirit adds up to more than the total of your 15 responses for the Acts of the Sinful Nature. From there you can move on into an examination of which sinful characteristics need to be removed and which positive ones need cultivating.

One other thing should be noted here. Christian liberty isn't a license to do everything you might like to do. If your "freedom" is in any way a stumbling block that interferes with the spiritual development of a weaker Christian, you should refrain from exercising it (1 Corinthians 8:9-13).

Sometimes traditions that no longer make sense *need* to be challenged (just as Paul challenged the tradition of circumcision). In many such cases, it is not new Christians who will feel threatened by more freedom, but people who have settled into an unthinking routine. We should keep our spiritual eyes open at all times for new opportunities to grow and experience all the freedom that Jesus has made available.

 KEY VERSE:
"The fruit of the Spirit is love, joy, peace, patience, kindness, goodness, faithfulness, gentleness and self-control. Against such things there is no law" (Galatians 5:22-23).

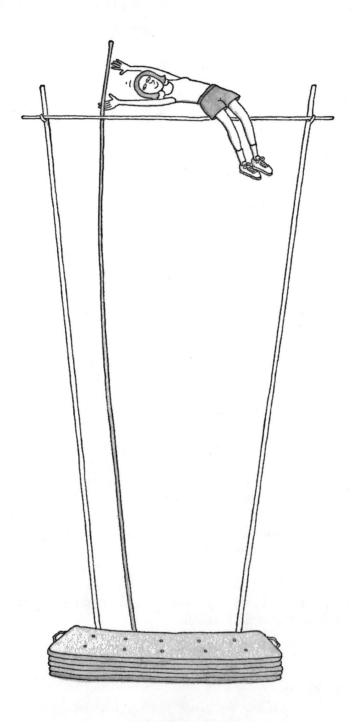

We never reach the point where we can say,
"No more goals to set."

5

GOALTENDING

(Book of Ephesians)

Kelly was at a concert. She and her husband had waited in line for hours to get good seats, and the tickets hadn't come cheaply. But she had heard lots of good things about this performer, so to her it was worth the time and money. As the lights went down and the crowd began to applaud, the musician stepped onto the stage. Then for the next hour and a half, he played scales. He played major scales and minor scales, fast scales and slow scales, standard scales and chromatic scales. He made playing scales look easy and he made playing scales look hard.

Soon Kelly was about to go crazy humming to herself: Do, re, mi, fa, sol, la, ti, do. Do, ti, la, sol, fa, mi, re, do. When the concert was over, many of the people were booing (of the few who were still there). But the artist called for silence and explained: "You see, when I was a child and had the desire to be a musician, I set a goal for myself. I knew how important it is to be able to play scales well, and I dreamed of mastering them. I hope you've enjoyed the results of my many years of effort."

Since the concert was such a disappointment, Kelly decided a change of pace was in order. So the next day she decided to watch a friend run in a local 10K race. She got a good position at the starting line and watched the participants take off at the crack of the gun. When they got out of sight, she drove to the finish line and waited.

Kelly saw dozens of people come panting across the line, but her friend never showed. She gave him a call that night and he told her, "Oh, I never expected to finish. When I took up running, I couldn't even run a mile without stopping. So I made it my goal to be able to run three miles. After a week or so I had reached the standard I had set for myself, and I've been running three miles every day since. My times are getting better too. But when I tried to run the 10K, I gave out at about the three-mile point."

Kelly refrained from telling her friend exactly what she thought of his strategy. After all, she would have to see him the next day at church. The thought of church reminded her that there was something her teacher had asked the young adult class to read for Sunday School. *Nah, forget it,* she thought. *I know as much as anybody else.*

Kelly spent the evening watching TV and never once considered the connection between herself, the musician, and her runner friend.

The End.

....

Do you see any similarities between the previous three characters? And if you can identify Kelly's problem, can you think of any ways the same problem affects *you?*

In this session we want to turn our attention to goal-setting. It seems that in most areas of life, the normal pattern is to set a reasonable goal, achieve it, and then set another more challenging goal. When you play the guitar, first you learn the chords. But after you learn some chords, you learn to put them together in the right arrangement to sound like a song. Then you work on strumming and picking. Then you discover new chords and alternate fingerings. And if you keep setting more challenging goals, before you know it you're playing along with Eric Clapton or Andrés Segovia.

When you're young, your parents and teachers get you started on learning the alphabet and counting to 100. But after you finally achieve those goals, you find that you can do a whole lot more stuff with letters and numbers. (You can even misuse them by putting together phrases like, "whole lot more stuff.")

When it comes to areas like education, music, athletics, and such, we instinctively raise our goals as soon as we have achieved a certain level of proficiency. Yet when it comes to spiritual things, we assume that if we haven't killed anyone this week, we're still doing OK. As we move into the Book of Ephesians, we are going to be challenged to crawl out of any spiritual ruts we may be in.

 JOURNEY ONWARD

The city of Ephesus was located in what is now Turkey. It was an important city because several trade routes intersected there. In Ephesus was a temple dedicated to the goddess Artemis (Diana). You may remember that Paul had gotten in trouble for preaching about Christianity in Ephesus because the craftsmen who made silver statues of Artemis were afraid of losing business (Acts 19:23-41).

As Paul wrote his letters to the Corinthians and the Galatians, he regularly addressed key problems those churches were facing. That didn't happen in his letter to the Ephesians. He refers to no specific problems as he addressed them. (Some people suggest that this letter was written to be circulated to a number of churches in addition to the one in Ephesus.) But throughout the letter, Paul challenged his readers to think big and strive for excellence in ways that perhaps they had never thought of before.

Read Ephesians 1:1-23.
After a short salutation (Ephesians 1:1-2), Paul moved directly into his message. He began by reminding the Ephesians of their importance to God. What has God done for His people? (1:3-6)

What does God provide as a free gift to us ("in accordance with the riches of [His] grace")? (1:7-8)

God has revealed to us what His will is — which was originally a "mystery." What is God planning to do? (1:9-10)

How does God "mark" His people? (1:11-14)

Getting Personal — *Have you been "marked" by God?*

When Paul heard about the faith of the Ephesians, he rejoiced and gave thanks to God (1:15-16). He also prayed for them (1:17). What three things did he request on their behalf? (1:18-19)

The power that Paul spoke of was no small thing. What had it accomplished in the past? (1:19-21)

What was the end result of God's previous display of His power? (1:22-23)

Before and After
Read Ephesians 2:1-22.
After his account of the things God had done for His people, Paul reminded them of how far they had already come. What was their starting point? (2:1)

What title is Satan given in this passage? (2:2)

What is the status of someone who has not yet believed in Jesus? (2:3)

How does a personal relationship with Christ change that status? (2:4-6)

Getting Personal—*How has a personal relationship with Christ affected your status with God?*

With such a dramatic and delightful difference in "Before Jesus" status and "After Jesus" status, it must be pretty hard to go from one to the other, right? Explain your answer (2:7-9).

Why did God create us in the first place? (2:10)

Before Jesus' death, there was massive tension between the Jews and Gentiles. How was that nonproductive relationship altered through the death and resurrection of Jesus? (2:11-18)

Paul used a couple of illustrations to demonstrate what he was saying. Since most of the Ephesians would have been non-Jewish, he first said that it was as if they had earned "citizenship" privileges entitling them to live near God and His people (2:12, 19). In what other way did Paul symbolize the new era of togetherness that God had in mind for the Jews and Gentiles? (2:19-22)

Good News for Gentiles
Read Ephesians 3:1-21.
Ephesians was probably written while Paul was under house arrest in Rome (Acts 28:16, 30-31). What is one of the clues that he gave to his location? (Ephesians 3:1)

As in his previous letters, Paul provided a short defense of his role as an apostle (3:2-6). When Paul had written the Corinthians, he had referred to himself as "the least of the apostles" (1 Corinthians 15:9). Do you think his opinion of himself had changed any during the past five years or so? Explain (Ephesians 3:7-9).

Do you think Paul was looking for sympathy as he wrote to the Ephesians (probably from a guarded room)? (3:10-13)

Paul soon shifted the focus from what God had done for him to what God could do for the readers of his letter. What hard-to-comprehend concept did he want them (and us) to grasp? (3:14-19)

Getting Personal — *Have you fully comprehended what God has done for you?*

What's another good reason to add to our lists of why we should give glory to God? (3:20-21)

Read Ephesians 4:1-6.
The logical result of receiving the love of Christ is to return it. And we show our love for God by being a unified church body. Unity cannot be taken lightly or ignored. What things did Paul say that there is just "one" of? (4:1-6)

Gifts and Goals
Read Ephesians 4:7-24.
Paul emphasized that unity is achieved by having each of the individuals in the church use his or her spiritual gift(s) for the good of the whole. (He expressed this same truth to the Romans and Corinthians.) Paul painted a verbal picture of Jesus as a victorious military leader who gives gifts to those who are on His side. And he explained that the reason Jesus is able to "ascend" and claim victory is because He first "descended" (4:8-10).

There are a few different opinions as to what verse 9 means when it says that Jesus "descended to the lower, earthly regions." Some believe this refers to Jesus' coming to earth in the first place. Others theorize that Jesus descended into hades between His death and resurrection. And a third interpretation is that Jesus "descended" into the grave at His burial and then was resurrected. This is one of those passages that might be good to discuss with your pastor and see what his interpretation is. But the main point is clear: Because of what Jesus has done, He is now victorious and responsible for the assigning of gifts as He sees fit. For what purpose does He give the gifts? (4:11-13)

Getting Personal — *Has Jesus assigned you one of these gifts?*

And as we use our gifts to interact with each other, it is certainly essential that we speak the truth. Yet telling the truth is not enough in and of itself. Exactly *how* should we present the truth? (4:14-16)

What happens to people who harden their hearts to God? (4:17-19)

Read Ephesians 4:25–5:4.
Paul insisted that Christians must not live like non-Christians (4:17). He explains that we have a whole new self. The general goal for our new self is simple: Be like God (4:20-24). But Paul didn't leave us to struggle with that general rule. He expounded a little and came up with several very specific goals for which we should strive. As you read Ephesians 4:25–5:4, list all the goals that we should be working toward. (There are quite a few.)

Read Ephesians 5:5-21.
Why is it essential that we take our spiritual goals seriously and try to accomplish them all? (5:5-7)

Paul explained that we were once darkness, but as Christians we are light. (Jesus said the same thing [Matthew 5:14].) If you've been out working on your car at night, you may not notice most of the grease on your hands and dirt underneath your fingernails. But when you come into the light, those dirty spots become very apparent. Similarly, the "dirty" areas of our lives might not seem too bad when we're out in the world where everyone else is "dirty" too. But as we draw near to Jesus as Christians, those sinful areas should become obvious in the light of His purity. And we then have no excuse not to set our standards considerably higher and eliminate those things from our lives (5:8-14).

Some people try to handle life by filling up with wine or other intoxicating beverages. But as Christians, we should try to fill up with something even more potent. What? (Or more precisely, who?) (5:15-20)

Getting Personal — *Other than alcohol, drugs, or food, what substitute do you use to help you handle life? How does this passage make you feel?*

Read Ephesians 5:22–6:12.
As we begin to set higher goals for ourselves and mature as Christians, one result is submission to each other. The biblical concept of submission is not what you might think. It doesn't mean that in a relationship one person is the absolute all-powerful master while the submissive person is the please-walk-all-over-me slave. A good example of biblical submission is found in 1 Corinthians 15:28, which states that Jesus "will be made subject" to God the Father. No single Person of the Trinity (Father, Son, and Holy Spirit) is either superior or inferior to the other two. But in their functions it is possible for one of the members to submit to the others. In no way does

submission suggest inferiority. Rather it makes possible an orderliness so the church can function effectively. How can each of the following groups of people demonstrate Christian submission in their relationships?

❑ Wives (5:22-24)

❑ Husbands (5:25-33)

❑ Children (6:1-3)

❑ Parents (6:4)

❑ Slaves (and perhaps employees as well?) (6:5-8)

❑ Masters (and bosses?) (6:9)

Getting Personal — *What is your definition of submission? Are you expressing a submissive spirit in all your relationships?*

Developing relationships that work is not just a nice thing to do. It is essential for Christians, because whether we realize it or not, we're in a battle. Who are our opponents? (6:10-12)

Read Ephesians 6:13-24.
We need to arm ourselves for this battle. But since our foes aren't flesh and blood, we need a special kind of protection. Paul compared the "armor" of God to that worn by soldiers. Review Ephesians 6:13-17 and write down which spiritual characteristics we need to possess to serve the function of each piece of armor that is listed.

❑ Belt

❑ Breastplate

❑ Footgear

❑ Shield

❑ Helmet

❑ Sword

And how should we supplement our "fighting" as Christians? (6:18)

Getting Personal — *What part of your armor is in the best shape? The worst shape?*

Some people point out that Paul mentioned no protection for our backs. If Christians try to run or hide from spiritual conflict, they become more vulnerable. We must learn to stand firm and move forward, using all of the available weapons and protection with which God provides us.

What was Paul's final request of the Ephesians? (6:19-20)

Paul's conclusion to his letter was brief (6:21-23), as was his opening. If indeed this letter was written to be circulated to other churches, it makes sense that it wouldn't contain a lot of personal greetings like many of his other letters do. But after the amount of solid content he provided, Paul didn't really need to say much more.

 JOURNEY INWARD

The Book of Ephesians gives us a lot to think about and respond to. It is filled with descriptions of the glory of God and the many things He makes available to us. It states clearly our undeserving status, and the degree of

God's grace that saved us while we were dead in our sin. And it describes how far we've already come as Christians, thanks to the presence of the Holy Spirit in our lives. But Ephesians also lets us know that we never reach the point where we can say, "Oh, good. I'm finally perfect, so I can quit trying so hard to improve myself." Consequently, when we reach one level of maturity, we need to strive for another, higher one. So it is important that we consider the need for **goal-setting** (and perhaps frequent revision of our goals).

For each of the following areas of your life, first list a goal that you have already accomplished in that area. After you've done that, list a current goal you have. (If you can't immediately think of a current goal, it's probably an indication that you're not continuing to grow in that area.) One example has been included to get you started.

EDUCATION/SPECIAL INTEREST GOALS (College, GPA, hobbies, etc.)

❏ Past goal—I wanted to take a computer course last year to improve my skills and job opportunities, and I did.

❏ Present goal—I want to take voice lessons so I can do a better job in the church choir.

❏ Past goal

❏ Present goal

CAREER GOALS (Jobs, interests, books you need to read, etc.)

❏ Past goal

❏ Present goal

PHYSICAL GOALS (Exercise plans, diet, sports activities, etc.)

❏ Past goal

❏ Present goal

FAMILY GOALS (Children, family activities, etc.)

❏ Past goal

❏ Present goal

SPIRITUAL GOALS (Relationships, involvement with church, discipline, etc.) These are important, so do a couple. If you have problems coming up with something, you only need to skim through Ephesians one more time and pick something that applies to you.

❏ Past goal

❏ Past goal

❏ Present goal

❏ Present goal

You'll probably come up with additional goals later, when you aren't even thinking about Paul, Ephesians, or spiritual things. But be sure to write them down anyway. Each and every area that comes to your mind is something you should be working on. In fact, as you learn to set better goals for yourself, your list is likely to become longer rather than shorter. And that's perfectly fine. It means you're focusing on overcoming the things that prevent you from becoming everything God wants you to be.

Our ultimate goal, in a word, should be Christlikeness. And we should devote our whole lives toward coming ever closer to that ultimate goal. As we "tend" to the things that help us achieve that goal, we will discover that this particular kind of goaltending will be the best investment of our time we've ever experienced. As we feel ourselves drawing closer to Jesus, the perception is that He is drawing nearer to us. And that's a sensation you never want to let come to an end.

 KEY VERSE:

"It is by grace you have been saved, through faith—and this not from yourselves, it is the gift of God—not by works, so that no one can boast. For we are God's workmanship, created in Christ Jesus to do good works, which God prepared in advance for us to do" (Ephesians 2:8-10).

What's the healthy way to respond to this situation?

6

ATTITUDES OF GRATITUDE

(Book of Philippians)

After saving your money for many months, you're finally able to afford the down payment on the red convertible you've been wanting since, well, ever since you can remember. You can't help but think back through all the things you sacrificed—the lunches you skipped, the extra weekend job you took, the trips to the mall where everyone except you left with their arms full of packages. But as you gaze at your brand-new car, your efforts now seem worthwhile.

All goes well during the first week. Your red car gives you a wonderful sense of freedom. You don't have to ride the commuter bus to work. You and the family can take an afternoon drive with the top down. And you're pleased that you made such a wise purchase.

But then, about 10 days later, you come home from a business trip and find that your car has been in a wreck. It's spotted with dirt, and mud is caked underneath the accordion-like fender. The antenna is bent. A couple of dents and scratches are obvious, and who knows how many more you'll find when you get it cleaned up. At this point, what would you be thinking? (Check the most appropriate response.)

❏ *Well, look at that. Someone in my family wrecked my car. What a shame.*
❏ *Well, look at that. Someone in my family wrecked my car. I certainly hope whoever did it wasn't hurt.*
❏ *Well, look at that. Someone in my family wrecked my car. I'm going to hunt him down and kill him.*

As you calmly inquire into the source of your car's distress, your spouse tells you that your son, Barry, had volunteered to drive for a youth group trip that day. His own jalopy wasn't running, and he "didn't think you'd mind" if he took your car. However, your spouse didn't know Barry would go driving through the woods, try jumping the car over some logs in the forest, or organize a "demolition derby" to end the day. And "the poor dear" was so tired when he got in that your spouse let him go right to bed. But don't worry, Barry's going to clean up your car first thing in the morning. What would you do?

☐ *Thank your spouse for using her/his best judgment on your behalf, since you weren't there.*
☐ *Explain to your spouse that perhaps she/he exceeded her/his rights by allowing your son to even touch the car.*
☐ *Scream incoherently at the top of your lungs until you lose your voice.*

The next morning you are up early to stake out the milk and cereal, knowing that your son will eventually come for his daily feeding frenzy. When he finally shows, you slip up behind him. And when he turns around, he's staring into your folded arms. At this point, what do you say?

☐ *Don't worry about the car, kid. I was young once myself. But perhaps next time you could check with me first.*
☐ *I want you to go outside right now and get my car cleaned up.*
☐ *OK, here's the way it's going to be, you little twerp. You are my slave until you earn enough money to pay for the damage.*

By this time, you've probably suspected that you're about to hear how you're supposed to be more patient and understanding when things go wrong. And you're probably getting ready to say, "Don't tell me I shouldn't get a little ticked off in situations like the ones described here! I'm only human. People have every right to confront others about things that make them upset."

Yes, sometimes confrontational action is indeed necessary. Yet perhaps it isn't required nearly as often as we choose to use it. And as you go through the Book of Philippians in this session, you will see that there is a healthier way to respond to most of your problems than with anger and conflict.

JOURNEY ONWARD

Philippians is another of the letters that Paul wrote from prison (more than likely, during his two-year confinement in Rome [Acts 28:30]). And Paul had done some time in Philippi as well. You may remember how he and Silas had been in the Philippian jail when an enormous earthquake caused everyone's chains to come loose and all the doors to be opened. Yet none of the prisoners escaped, and Paul and Silas helped the jailer and his family discover the truth about Jesus and Christianity (Acts 16:25-34). As you read his letter, it will become obvious that Paul had some very special feelings for the church people in Philippi.

Read Philippians 1:1-30.
Again, Timothy was apparently nearby when Paul wrote (Philippians 1:1-2). What emotions did Paul feel as he thought of the Philippian church? Why? (1:3-5)

What confidence did Paul have in regard to the Philippians? (1:6)

How did Paul's circumstances (being in prison) affect his attitude toward his friends in Philippi? (1:7-8)

What was Paul's prayer for the Philippians? (1:9-11)

How had Paul's imprisonment affected the spread of the Gospel in his area? (1:12-14)

You know by now that everything Paul did was out of pure motives and his genuine love for God. Yet while he was in prison, a lot of people were spreading the Gospel more to make a name for themselves than for any other reason. What was Paul's attitude toward such people? Why? (1:15-18)

Getting Personal — *Do you have pure motives when you share the Gospel with others?*

Paul never wanted to be ashamed of his attitude toward Jesus. In fact, he was committed to exalting Christ — no matter what. Preferably, his *life* would continue to bring glory to Jesus. But if it ever got to such a point, Paul was ready to have his *death* bring glory to Jesus as well (1:19-20). How did Paul feel about life and death? (1:21-26)

Paul also challenged the Philippians to "stand firm in one spirit" as they continued to spread the Gospel. He noted similarities in their lives and his own. What did Paul say went along with a person's belief in Jesus? (1:27-30)

Read Philippians 2:1-4.
But as soon as Paul mentioned the "down side" of Christianity, he immediately listed a number of tremendous benefits of being united with Jesus. What are they? (2:1)

And since those things are available to Christians, what are we able to do? (2:2-4)

Attitude Adjustment

We hear a lot about how our actions should be unquestionable. So far in this book we've already seen the importance of showing kindness to one another, using spiritual gifts to work together as one body, bearing one another's burdens, and so forth. But here Paul went straight to the source of our actions—our attitudes. Unless our attitudes are right, our actions will always be forced and insincere.

Read Philippians 2:5-30.

Just as Jesus is the model for our actions, so also is He the model for our attitudes. What is the standard He has set for the kind of attitude we should develop? Be specific (2:5-8).

Getting Personal—*How does your own attitude toward caring for others measure up against the standard set by Jesus?*

What was the result of Jesus' model attitude? (2:9-11)

Most of us are going to fall a little short of Jesus' example. So what does Paul advise us to do, and what do you think he meant? As you answer, keep in mind that salvation is a free gift from God (2:12-13).

Just so his last statement wouldn't be misunderstood, Paul expressed himself more clearly: "Do everything without complaining or arguing" (2:14). He never said that this will be easy or convenient. But when you learn to do this, you are going to stand out in a world full of petty, complaining people. Exactly how much are you going to stand out? (2:14-16)

Getting Personal—*When and where do you do your most complaining and arguing?*

Realizing that his jail sentence could possibly become a death sentence, Paul had every reason to be fearful or negative. Yet in trying to build up the Philippians, he mentioned the possibility of his death in the context of a "drink offering" (2:17). In the Old Testament, the priests were to offer each day a lamb in the morning and another at twilight. With each lamb was presented a "grain offering" composed of fine flour and oil, and a "drink offering" of wine which was poured on the sacrifice (Exodus 29:38-41).

Even if Paul's life ended with his being "poured out" in sacrifice, he recognized that the "lamb" of the offering was the active faith of the Philippians. How did that make him feel? (Philippians 2:17-18)

Getting Personal—*Identify several people you have known who have "poured out" their lives in sacrifice for others.*

While he was passing out praise to the Philippians, Paul also had some glowing words for a couple of the people who were in Rome with him. What good things did Paul have to say about Timothy? (2:19-24)

The other person was a man named Epaphroditus. (Surely this guy had a nickname among his friends.) What kind of person was he? (2:25-30)

Read Philippians 3:1-19.
Paul wanted the Philippians to rejoice (3:1). Sure, they had problems. They were being subjected to the same teachings of the Judaizers that the Galatians were facing. Paul told them to be smart and watch out for the false teachings of these guys, but they could rejoice in the Lord while doing so (3:1-3). If Paul hadn't been such a strong Christian, do you think he would have made a good Judaizer? Explain (3:4-6).

But even though Paul had some pretty good credentials, how did he feel about his past accomplishments? (3:7-9)

We talked about our goals in the last session. But here Paul states one of the driving goals of *his* life. What was it? (3:10-11)

What was Paul's attitude as he worked toward his goal? (3:12-16)

Getting Personal — *Where do you picture yourself in the race for the prize? What prize are you after? How do you plan to reach your goal?*

Paul's attitude is one that should be imitated. Many people give up much too quickly in their pursuit of a godly lifestyle. They get caught up in looking all around them or behind them instead of seeing what is *before* them. What is the situation of those who refuse to seek the things of God? (3:17-19)

Read Philippians 3:20–4:1.
What is one reason why a Christian lifestyle is so much different than a non-Christian one? (3:20–4:1)

Getting Specific
Read Philippians 4:2-23.
Paul illustrated this general principle with a specific example. He had once worked with two ladies in the Philippian church: Euodia and Syntyche. But apparently these two ladies were the source of a recent (and major) conflict in Philippi, and Paul publicly appealed to them to settle their differences (4:2-3). What alternative did he suggest rather than squabbling over our disagreements? (4:4-5)

Getting Personal — *How do you cope with conflict?*

How can we learn to do this? (4:6-7)

Since our attitudes influence our actions, that's the place we need to start. So how do we bring our attitudes into line? (4:8)

And when we learn to do this, what is a promised result that should also drastically affect our actions? (4:9)

While Paul wanted to make sure the Philippian church was still motivated to strive for perfection, he knew they were off to a good start. He had some kind words to say to them about their willingness to give to his ministry (4:10). Of course, most of us could find good things to say about people who give us money. But do you think that's why Paul was thankful for the giving spirit of the Philippians? Explain (4:11-13).

To what extent had the Philippian church exemplified a giving attitude? (4:14-18)

And because they were such good givers, what did Paul promise them? (4:19-20)

In closing, Paul was able to send greetings from some different people than those he has referred to in previous letters. Who were included in Paul's new circle of friends? (4:21-23)

So what do you think? If someone had borrowed and damaged Paul's new red convertible, do you think he would have responded in the same way you did in this session's opening pages? Explain your answer.

JOURNEY INWARD

It's almost impossible for us to imagine someone under the guard of soldiers of the Roman Empire telling his friends to rejoice and follow his example. It's one thing to be joyful and motivated if you're out traveling and speaking to people in their churches. But Paul was unable to get feedback from these people, other than an occasional letter or message. His actions were pretty much confined to writing letters and sharing the Gospel with any of Caesar's servants he met. And for those actions to be so consistently positive, he must have had incredible insight into the importance of **attitudes.**

So far, this book has put an emphasis on the importance of godly actions. But now we need to be sure that first we have positive attitudes. Until we create attitudes that are rooted in Christian love, we don't really stand a chance to permanently avoid sinful actions.

As you consider your attitudes, make a list of things that you are required to do, yet that you really detest. Your list can include household chores, job headaches, PTA assignments, church activities, or anything else you can think of. Write those things below.

Now think for a moment: Do you hate to do these things because they are so terrible? Or do these things seem so terrible because you hate to do them so much? Be honest. In most cases, if we could alter our attitudes, the actual actions wouldn't be nearly so bad.

Now suppose that the Apostle Paul had to do the same things that are on your list. Do you think he would complain about them as much as you do? Perhaps he would. But if you don't think so, you need to figure out why his attitudes would be different than yours. He scatters several clues throughout Philippians that may at least partially help you understand his secret to positive attitudes.

CLUE #1—"Do nothing out of selfish ambition or vain conceit, but in humility consider others better than yourselves. Each of you should look not only to your own interests, but also to the interests of others" (2:3-4).

Does your problem with any of the items on your list stem from a lack of humility? Do you think you're "too good" to do some of those things? Do you have selfish motives for wanting to avoid some of them?

CLUE #2—"I consider everything a loss compared to the surpassing greatness of knowing Christ Jesus my Lord" (3:8).

Are the things on your list *really* important? Many of the things we complain about are "small stuff" that we should give little if any thought to. Do you allow anything to cause others to question your faith? If so, wouldn't it be better to quit complaining for that reason if for no other?

CLUE #3 — "Rejoice in the Lord always. I will say it again: Rejoice!" (4:4)

If you're rejoicing in the Lord always, you should be rejoicing during the activities you've listed. Do you? Do you think you should? And if you begin to do a little more rejoicing, do you think your attitude toward those things is going to improve?

CLUE #4 — "Whatever is true, whatever is noble, whatever is right, whatever is pure, whatever is lovely, whatever is admirable — if anything is excellent or praiseworthy — think about such things" (4:8).

As you perform the duties on your list, what are you thinking? Are your thoughts true, noble, right, etc.? How would positive thoughts affect the carrying out of those chores?

If you lived by the standards described in Paul's four clues, perhaps the things that really get to you now would no longer seem so horrible. (And if you look hard, you can probably find additional clues in the Book of Philippians.)

Get started this week. Select at least one starting point and work on it every day. Whether it involves cleaning up your thoughts, rejoicing more frequently, or whatever, it will be a strong start in getting your attitudes shaped up. And from there, your actions will fall into place.

 KEY VERSE:
"Your attitude should be the same as that of Christ Jesus: Who, being in very nature God, did not consider equality with God something to be grasped, but made Himself nothing, taking the very nature of a servant, being made in human likeness. And being found in appearance as a man, He humbled Himself and became obedient to death — even death on a cross!" (Philippians 2:5-8)

One of the worst things about lying is that we don't have an
easy way to tell when people aren't being straight with us.

7

THE WHOLE TRUTH,
AND NOTHING BUT THE TRUTH

(Book of Colossians)

You all know the story of Pinocchio—at least, the way his nose would grow every time he told a lie. Did you ever think how much simpler your life would be if there were an easy way to tell if people were lying? Consider some of the following possibilities. And imagine in each case that if the person tells a lie, his or her nose grows six inches.

❏ Witnesses in courtrooms would no longer have to place their hands on a Bible and swear to tell "the truth, the whole truth, and nothing but the truth." It would be obvious to the judge and jury if they were lying.

❏ Airport security personnel could quickly ask people if they were carrying any weapons or bombs. It would be a lot quicker to check noses than to search everyone's carry-on luggage, purses, pockets, and so forth.

❏ Internal Revenue Service employees would no longer need to go through a complex auditing process. They could just ask selected taxpayers if they had been honest while filling out their tax forms.

❏ Congressional committees to investigate crooked politicians would save a lot of time if the accused's nose was likely to grow on national TV. This would also save millions of the taxpayers' dollars.

❏ Retail stores (especially record stores) wouldn't need those magnetic detectors at the doors. As shoppers left, the store manager could ask them, "Hey, did you steal anything while you were in here?"

❏ Schoolteachers, for quizzes or term papers, could simply ask students, "Is this your own work, or did you cheat?"

❏ Kids could never again get by with lying to their parents and blaming their own accidents on siblings, pets, and so forth.

Now here's the hard question. In what situations would you be caught with a long nose? When are those times when you find it convenient or "necessary" to lie? Write those examples below.

We all know that *Pinocchio* is just a story. Expand-O-Noses could never really be developed (for which most of us breathe a big sigh of relief). Yet the fact that we aren't as likely to get caught in our lies shouldn't make lying any more acceptable to us. The Christian standard we profess has no room for telling lies to one another. But it seems that lying has become so common (and so tolerated) that it doesn't matter too much to us.

One of the worst things about lying is that we don't have any easy way to tell when people aren't being straight with us. It would be so easy if their noses started to grow. But since that's not going to happen, it's up to us to learn to separate truth from fiction when someone tells us something we aren't sure about. Sometimes it doesn't matter all that much. Yet at other times, unrecognized lies can be extremely harmful.

 JOURNEY ONWARD

The Book of Colossians was written to a group of people who were being lied to. It is another of the letters Paul sends from his prison in Rome, so all he can do is write to encourage the Colossians to try to expose the untruths that were being presented to them. These lies were definitely harmful because they dealt with the very basics of Christianity.

The Colossian church was being threatened by a different group of people than the Galatian church. You know about the philosophy of the Judaizers who were trying to pervert Christianity by insisting on maintaining many of the Old Testament requirements, such as circumcision. But the threat in Colosse was from a group of people who eventually became known as Gnostics (the G is silent). The teachings of Gnosticism were more prevalent in the second and third centuries, but this deceptive religion was taking root during the first century.

In his letter to the Colossian church, Paul only hints at the content of the

Gnostic teaching. But based on what he says and on what we know about later Gnostic teachings, it's not too hard to identify some of the lies of the Gnostics. They too had an Old Testament mind-set and stressed certain Jewish ceremonies and special days. They believed in secret, deeper knowledge, and people were subject to the "visions" of Gnostic leaders. They worshiped angels. They were very selective, restricting membership in their organization and encouraging those who belonged to feel superior. And, in probably their worst offense of all, they denied the deity of Jesus. (Simply put, they thought that Jesus was less than God.) As you read through this letter, you'll see that Paul addresses each of these points.

Read Colossians 1:1-14.
It didn't take him long, either. In his salutation, Paul emphasized two good characteristics of the people in Colosse. What were they? (Colossians 1:1-2)

And Paul reminded them that they weren't the only people around who had been strongly influenced by the Gospel of Jesus. Where else was the Gospel spreading? (1:3-6)

Consequently, the Colossians shouldn't have been so quick to doubt something that had so powerfully affected them. Paul may have never personally visited Colosse. So how was he so sure of their spiritual development? (1:7-8)

Even though Paul may never have seen the church in Colosse, how was he still involved with it? (1:9)

Getting Personal — *How do your prayers compare with Paul's in terms of intensity and thankfulness?*

Paul challenged the Colossians to live lives that pleased God. He also gave them a number of specific ways to do just that. What things did he recommend? (1:10-14)

Christ Above All
Read Colossians 1:15-29.
Salvation is like being snatched from the "dominion of darkness" (v. 13) and lovingly transported to the "kingdom of light" (v. 12). And salvation comes through only one Person—Jesus Christ, the Son of God. Because of the ultimate sacrifice made by Jesus to make our salvation possible, He deserves our love, praise, loyalty, thanksgiving, and more. Yet the Gnostics in Colosse were saying that Jesus wasn't really all that important. So in Paul's letter, he listed a number of "qualifications" of Jesus (as if He needs them). List the reasons Paul gives why Jesus deserves our complete praise.

Getting Personal — *What forces or people sometimes seem more powerful to you than Jesus Christ? How do you feel when you hear that even these things are subject to Jesus' authority?*

How much of God the Father is reflected in Jesus? (1:19-20)

What has Jesus done for you personally? (1:21-22)

Knowing the direction the Gnostic leaders were taking, what did Paul encourage the Colossians to do? (1:23)

Paul made the strange-sounding statement that, "I fill up in my flesh what is still lacking in regard to Christ's afflictions" (1:24). By this he didn't mean that Jesus had left anything lacking in His arrangement for our salvation. But Paul had indeed suffered to see that people throughout his part of the world heard the story of Jesus. Only in the fact that people may not have heard the Gospel can it be said to be "lacking." So what was Paul's personal goal? (1:24-29)

Getting Personal — *Is Paul's personal goal a reality in your life?*

Read Colossians 2:1-23.
How did Paul feel about the churches that he didn't start and hadn't yet visited? (2:1-5)

On what were the false teachings of the Gnostics based? (2:6-8)

But Christianity offers so much more. Look at Paul's comments in Colossians 2:9-10: In Christ is "all the fullness of the Deity" (everything God can possibly be). And *through* Christ, "you have been given fullness" (to become everything you can possibly be). With all this fullness that's available, who should want the empty doctrines of false teachers?

Paul also makes an interesting statement regarding circumcision. He says that Jesus has circumcised us, but not in the traditional Old Testament way. Instead of "putting off" a small piece of foreskin to make believers distinctive from nonbelievers, what has Jesus "put off" that serves the same purpose? (2:11)

What is the symbolic significance of baptism? (2:12)

Getting Personal—*Have you been baptized? What is the significance of your baptism to you? To others?*

How completely did Jesus put away the "written code" of the Old Testament law? Explain (2:13-15).

What things should we watch out for? (2:16-23)

(NOTE: Don't miss Paul's visual images of the law as a "shadow of the things that were to come" and of false teachers as people who have "lost connection with the Head." If you've ever seen a chicken running around with its head cut off, you can know exactly what Paul was talking about.)

Read Colossians 3:1-17.
In general, how can we avoid being misled by false teachers and their doctrines? (3:1-4)

Getting Personal — *Have you ever been misled by false teachers or doctrines? How did you escape their misleading?*

Specifically, what do we need to get rid of? (3:5-11)

Specifically, what do we need to acquire? (3:12-14)

It's one thing to have a mental knowledge of Jesus and what He has done for us. But what is the next step we need to take? (3:15)

As we take that next step, what will begin to take place in our lives? (3:16)

Toward what eventual goal should we all be working? (3:17)

Happy Homes
Read Colossians 3:18–4:18.

As with the Ephesians, Paul gave the Colossians some commonsense rules for living as Christians (3:18–4:1). Wives should submit to their husbands. Husbands should love their wives and avoid being nasty to them. Slaves should obey their masters. Masters should treat slaves fairly. Fathers shouldn't be too rough on their children. And children should obey their parents. (By the way, the Israelites had laws pertaining to excessively disobedient, stubborn, and rebellious children. The parents were to take such children to the town elders, who would stone them to death [Deuteronomy 21:18-21].)

What is the one of the keys to making sure that all these relationships work properly? (3:23-25)

What is another? (4:2)

Getting Personal — *How much do you pray for others in proportion to praying for your own concerns?*

What request did Paul make for himself? (4:3-4)

How should we treat those outside the church? (4:5)

We are challenged to "let your conversation be always full of grace, seasoned with salt, so that you may know how to answer everyone" (4:6). "Grace" brings to mind concepts such as undeserved assistance, charm, dignity, honor, and such. Salt provides taste and, during Paul's time, worked as a preservative by being rubbed into meat. With these things in mind, what do you think Paul was trying to tell us?

As Paul concluded his letter to the Colossians, he included quite a few personal greetings. He explained that he was sending a person named Tychicus (who had also been Paul's messenger to the church in Ephesus [Ephesians 6:21-22]). Why did Paul send Tychicus to Colosse? (Colossians 4:7-8)

Tychicus had a traveling companion named Onesimus, whom you will meet in Session 12 of this book. Paul also sent greetings from several people who were with him. One was a man named Aristarchus, who was mentioned in connection with Paul several times in the Book of Acts (19:29; 20:4; 27:2). Aristarchus was from Thessalonica, a city you'll hear more about in the next couple of sessions.

Also with Paul was John Mark, who wrote the Book of Mark. You may remember that Mark had been the source of conflict between Paul and Barnabas after their first missionary journey recorded in Acts (Acts 15:36-41). Paul was annoyed that Mark had "deserted" them. Do you think Paul and Mark were reconciled at this point? (Colossians 4:10)

Others whom Paul remembered to the Colossians were Justus, Epaphras, Luke, and Demas. Among these, Epaphras stands out. Besides being responsible for taking the Gospel to Colosse in the first place (1:7), what else was Epaphras doing for the Colossian church? (4:12-13)

In closing, Paul urged the Colossians, "Remember my chains" (4:18). Even though he was hundreds of miles away in a prison cell, he could think of and pray for the Colossians (most of whom he had never met). They could do the same for him. And the unity of the body of Christ could transcend all those boundaries for the good of the church. We have much to learn from this example.

 JOURNEY INWARD

But then, we have much to learn about a lot of things. From this Book of Colossians, we want to focus our thoughts on one essential area. Let's look for a few moments at the importance of **truth.**

The concept of truth is so broad that we can't do a complete study in the little bit of space that remains in this session. But we *can* pull out a few main observations and see how well we're doing in those specific areas.

For example, one thing that should be obvious from your study of Colossians is that *a definite standard of truth exists.* You will always be able to find certain people who believe that, "What's right for you may not be right for me." Their understanding of truth is something that is flexible. So when they consider spiritual things, they assume that God will be flexible and "grade on the curve," so to speak. But not so. God has clearly stated His truth, and has modeled it for us in the person of Jesus (who is "the way, the truth, and the life" [John 14:6]). In many cases where truth seems to be relative, the problem is that we just haven't looked hard enough for the answer. Or perhaps we haven't really wanted to know. Can you think of anything that you are having some doubts with at this point in your life — some "truths" you've been told that you aren't quite sure you believe? List anything you can think of in the space below.

A second thing we need to learn from Colossians is that *it's important to recognize truth when we see or hear it.* Even when we are convinced that truth exists, we don't always differentiate it from some of the clever lies that are directed our way. Just as the Gnostics were trying to get the Colossians to desert their true Christian faith, sometimes we are influenced by doctrines or people who are out to mislead us. If you know of any such people or ideas that threaten to interfere with your relationship with Jesus, list them below.

A third thing we should observe from Colossians is that *Christians should always be solid examples of truth.* In a world where truth often seems to be either unimportant or undiscovered, it is essential for those of us who know and recognize it to model it for others. We should stand out from others who feel the liberty to use little fibs, "white lies," exaggerations, flattery, and other methods of dodging the absolute truth. You had the opportunity at the beginning of this session to list some of the times you don't tell the truth.

Perhaps you were thinking of "small" offenses at that time. If you can think of any additional instances where you aren't exactly truthful, list them here.

Now that you've responded to the lessons on truth from the Book of Colossians, maybe you need to take additional action during the next week. For instance, if you had questions concerning the truth of certain areas of your life, you should do a little research on those questions. Talk to knowledgeable people in your church. Check out some good books. Spend some extra time in prayer, asking God to show you the truth on these matters (since He is the source of all truth).

You should also put in some extra prayer time if you came up with a list of influences that threaten to distract you from the real truth of Jesus Christ. Plan some definite actions to take so you can recognize the blinding lies of these influences.

And if you came up with some times when you frequently tell lies, you have a natural starting point for action right there. After going through this session, you should think twice the next time an untruth begins to come out of your mouth. At that very point, you need to remember to change your speech patterns until you learn to tell the truth at all times. But remember what you learned in Ephesians. It's not enough just to tell the truth. You must learn to speak "the truth in love" (Ephesians 4:15). It's easy enough to say, "We should always tell the truth." But when we start trying to actually do it, we discover that it's very difficult. The only way we'll ever be able to model a completely truthful life is to stay close to the source of truth. As Jesus provides the strength and courage to eliminate all untruth from our lives, we'll be the better for it. And that's no lie.

 KEY VERSE:

"Whatever you do, whether in word or deed, do it all in the name of the Lord Jesus, giving thanks to God the Father through Him" (Colossians 3:17).

Robert seemed to only care about himself, overlooking the fact that his actions might be recorded.

8

COME BACK
TO SEE US

(Book of 1 Thessalonians)

You have just been hired by a man to work in his store. He has also hired an employee named Robert. The store is a small deli—the kind with loyal customers who keep coming because they know what to expect. And after a month, you and Robert have more or less learned your jobs well.

One day your boss calls you both into his office and explains that he's going away for a while. He plans to attend an out-of-town Restaurateur's Convention, visit some family members, and then do some business that should eventually help the deli. But he has complete confidence that you and Robert can keep the store going during his absence.

He shows the two of you how to take inventory, reorder whatever you need, open and lock up, check in the vendors, take each day's deposit to the bank, balance the books, and do everything else you should need to know. As he gets in his car to leave, his last words are, "Take good care of my store. I'm leaving her in your hands."

You are thinking what a great opportunity this will be to show that you are capable of running a business on your own. But Robert apparently doesn't share your feelings. He looks over at you with a gleam in his eye.

The first week went smoothly. The customers were surprised that your boss had left, but they warmed up to you pretty soon. You soon began to call most of the regulars by name, and you were really getting into the job. Robert seemed a little withdrawn, but otherwise, all was fine.

After two weeks, your boss hadn't returned. He hadn't even called. During the third week, Robert came in on Monday and announced, "I need some time off. I'm taking a couple of days." He then walked out without even giving you time to argue. And though it was much harder to do the work of two people, you got by.

Robert didn't show till the following Monday. And when he did, he had a couple of six-packs with him. You asked him what he thought he was doing, but he was belligerent and told you it was none of your business. He spent the day eating whatever he wanted right off the shelves without paying for anything. He always had a can of beer in one hand. And whenever a customer came in, Robert would glare at the person as if he or she were really bothering him. Each day that week, Robert seemed to get worse. Even though he was there, you still had to do all the work. It was almost as if he thought you were his slave or something.

When Robert started to insult customers to their faces, most of them stopped coming in. You had to cut back on orders because stuff was going bad before you could sell it. And whenever you tried to talk to Robert about his attitude, he would just say, "Look, it's obvious that the old man's not coming back. It's you and me. You can do what you want, but just shut your face and leave me alone."

You wanted to get in touch with the owner, but he had left no forwarding numbers. You feared the worst. He would come back, see what had happened to his store, and wouldn't even ask questions. You and Robert would both be out the door. You needed the money from this job, and would be in sorry shape if you lost it. So you began to dread the day your boss would show up.

In the sixth week, you got a call at the store while Robert was out running around with his friends (with money he had taken out of the register). It was your boss. He explained that he had been detained but was on his way home. He wanted a favor from you. Would you take the key hidden in a certain drawer, unlock a particular panel in his office, and insert a new videotape in the hidden camera? He explained that one of his friends had been coming in at night to do this, but was unable to this time.

You knew nothing about a hidden camera, and were terrified to think that your actions might have been recorded. Your boss assured you that indeed you *were* on "candid" camera and had shown yourself to be trustworthy. Robert, on the other hand, would soon be visited by the police and made to pay for his misdeeds.

You probably know some people like Robert who seem to care only about themselves. How do you respond to such people? Do you maintain your own integrity, or do you occasionally let them talk you into things that you don't really want to do? Come on, be honest. Think of specific examples and write your comments below.

 JOURNEY ONWARD

We will almost always cause ourselves problems if we put too much focus on the present and not enough on the future. Present circumstances and situations are important, of course, but they should be in the context of things to come.

In this session you will cover the Book of 1 Thessalonians. Even though you've already been through several of Paul's letters, this one is probably the first or second he wrote chronologically. As a historical note, Thessalonica was a prosperous city, the largest city in Macedonia, and the capital of its province. Paul, Silas, and Timothy had all spent some time teaching in Thessalonica.

Read 1 Thessalonians 1:1-10.
In Session 6, we considered the connection between attitudes and actions. As Paul opens his letter to the Thessalonian church, he mentions three actions they had taken and the attitudes that had inspired them. What did he list? (1 Thessalonians 1:1-3)

How had Paul become convinced of the sincerity of the faith of the Thessalonians? List all the reasons you can find (1:4-6).

Getting Personal — *How are others convinced of your sincerity of faith?*

Because the Thessalonians had responded to the Gospel with such devotion, what had happened? (1:7-10)

It seemed that the willingness of the Thessalonians to respond to the Gospel had special significance to Paul. You may remember from the Book of Acts how for a long time it seemed that all Paul faced was opposition. He went to Thessalonica from Philippi, where he had been dragged before the authorities for casting an evil spirit out of a slave girl, stripped and severely beaten, and finally was jailed with his feet in stocks (Acts 16:16-24). His trip to Thessalonica wasn't completely peachy, but it was noted that "some of the Jews were persuaded and joined Paul and Silas, as did a large number of God-fearing Greeks and not a few prominent women" (Acts 17:4).

Read 1 Thessalonians 2:1-16.
What had motivated Paul to present the Gospel message in Thessalonica, even though he had just been run out of Philippi? (1 Thessalonians 2:1-2)

You might think that Paul would be a little desperate to have people listen to him after so many others hadn't. Yet Paul avoided many of the "tricks" of public speaking as he presented the Gospel to the Thessalonians. What were some of the tactics that he *didn't* use? (2:3-5)

How *did* Paul present the Gospel? (2:6-7)

Getting Personal — *What presentations of the Gospel really turn you off?*

And in addition to the Gospel, what did Paul share with the Thessalonians? (2:8)

Describe Paul's behavior while he was in Thessalonica (2:9-12).

If you had been in Paul's place, don't you think you would have been thankful if the Thessalonians had responded to your words? After all the opposition you had encountered in other places, wouldn't you tend to think: *I've finally done some good here!* Well, Paul was thankful, but not for exactly the same reason. Why did Paul give thanks in regard to the Thessalonians? (2:13)

What did the church in Thessalonica have in common with the churches in Judea? (2:14-16)

If you're reading closely, you may see that Paul is dropping little clues that reveal the direction he is heading. In 1:10 he had referred to "Jesus, who rescues us from the coming wrath." In 2:16 he said in regard to ungodly people: "The wrath of God has come upon them at last." Keep these things in mind. You will read more specifics in 1 Thessalonians 4–5.

Homesick for Thessalonica
Read 1 Thessalonians 2:17-20.
Why did Paul say he couldn't get back to visit Thessalonica again? (2:17-18)

It wasn't that Paul didn't want to go back to see them. In fact, how did he describe the people in the church at Thessalonica? (2:19-20)

Getting Personal — *Do you ever get homesick for old Christian friends?*

Read 1 Thessalonians 3:1-13.
When Paul found he couldn't return to Thessalonica, what arrangements did he make instead? (3:1-5)

What kind of report did Paul receive about the Thessalonian church? (3:6)

How did the report from Thessalonica affect Paul's mood? (3:7-9)

Getting Personal — *How have you been encouraged by someone else's faith?*

Did the report from Thessalonica lessen Paul's desire to visit? Explain (3:10-13).

And there Paul goes again — talking about "when our Lord Jesus comes with all His holy ones" (3:13). Hold that thought. You're about to get to that important topic.

Read 1 Thessalonians 4:1-12.

But first Paul wanted to remind us of the importance of sanctification. If you do not recall the significance of being sanctified, the basic idea is that after God justifies us (forgives our sins and declares us righteous), He then sanctifies us (sets us apart from the rest of the sinful world for His use.) Sanctification is very closely related to holiness. Paul reminded us that it is clearly God's will that we be sanctified. In what ways should we be "set apart"? (4:1-6)

It's admirable when we make a conscientious attempt to set ourselves apart from the world. But what's a better reason to keep trying to improve our levels of holiness? (4:6-8)

As you start to lead a sanctified life, obey God, and love one another, is it then OK to run on "automatic pilot" and stop trying so hard? Explain (4:9-10).

Getting Personal — *How would you explain the concept of sanctification to a person who thinks he can do anything he wants, as long as it feels good and no one gets hurt?*

How did Paul suggest that we can keep from being dependent on others and win the respect of non-Christians? (4:11-12)

The Rapture
Read 1 Thessalonians 4:13-18.
While he was talking about the differences between Christians and non-Christians, Paul began to address the issue he had been hinting at throughout this letter. He says that one of the best things about being a Christian is the way Christians can learn to handle death. He didn't want the Thessalonians to be "ignorant" and to grieve for their loved ones as if there were no hope (4:13). Of course we're going to grieve when someone close to us dies, but we have a confidence that death is not the end. And then Paul launched into his teachings concerning the "Rapture" of the church and the last days. (Nowhere in the Bible is this event called the Rapture. The word comes from the Latin *rapturo*, meaning "caught up.")

We can make two observations about Paul's statement, "Jesus died." First, the statement that Jesus died is in contrast to the one that says we who believe "fall asleep." The difference is that when Jesus died (before He rose again), He experienced death in a way we will never have to. Second, Paul says that Jesus "died" instead of "was killed." Though the circumstances of His death involved a Roman death sentence, the Bible is very clear that Jesus voluntarily laid down His life for us. And His death makes possible our own resurrection after we die.

Who will be the first to be "caught up" into heaven—the Christians living on earth or those who have already died? (4:13-18)

Is this going to be a secretive event, or one that is apparent to everyone? Explain your answer (4:16).

After we are taken up to be with God, how long will we get to stay with Him? (4:17)

Should we be frightened by this knowledge? (4:18)

Getting Personal—*How does this passage help you deal with the fear of death?*

The Day of the Lord
Read 1 Thessalonians 5:1-28.

Another big event that follows the Rapture is the "Day of the Lord." This period of time will be covered more comprehensively in *Home at Last* (Book #4) of this **BibleLog for Adults Series** when you study the Book of Revelation. But there are some valuable clues to help us understand the Day of the Lord right here in 1 Thessalonians.

How well prepared will the world be for Jesus' return to earth? (5:1-3)

Notice that when Paul described the Rapture, he keeps saying "we" will do so-and-so. But as he began to talk about the Day of the Lord, he referred to other people and didn't seem to include himself. Again, when we get to Revelation, we will look at some different interpretations of the order of events for this turbulent time. In the meantime, this is another good passage to discuss with your pastor and see what he thinks.

Yet one thing remains clear: the attitude Christians are to have regarding the Day of the Lord. How should we anticipate it? Why? (5:4-8)

Why don't we need to fear God's wrath? (5:9-11)

Paul concluded his letter with a list of things we should be doing as we anticipate the return of Jesus. Read through his list in 5:12-22, and transfer each of Paul's commands to one of the columns below, depending on whether or not you're doing as he instructed.

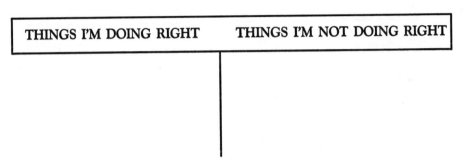

THINGS I'M DOING RIGHT	THINGS I'M NOT DOING RIGHT

Paul closed his letter with a prayer that God will "sanctify you through and through" (5:23-28). As we anticipate the certain and eventual return of Jesus, we need to allow God to have control over more of our lives each day until we can say our "whole spirit, soul and body [is] kept blameless at the coming of our Lord Jesus Christ" (5:23).

 JOURNEY INWARD

Paul surely gave us plenty to consider in this session. Perhaps the best thing we can do right now is to contemplate how well we are prepared for **the second coming of Jesus.**

Paul wrote as if he fully expected Jesus to return during his lifetime (4:13-18). And as you have seen, Paul lived his life in such a way that he wouldn't need to be ashamed of anything if Jesus *did* suddenly call him up to heaven with the rest of the Christians.

Sure, it's about 2,000 years later, but today's date doesn't make Jesus' return any less certain. When we get to Peter's books of the Bible, we'll find out that God isn't being slow. Rather, He's being patient because He doesn't want anyone to perish (2 Peter 3:9). Perhaps it will be another 2,000 years before Jesus returns. But then, it *could* be before you read to the end of the next sentence. So the challenge for this session is simple: We need to learn to live as if Jesus might return at any minute, because He might. We won't know when it's going to happen.

But let's suppose we *did* know. Imagine that you are absolutely sure that Jesus would call all Christians into heaven one week from today. With that knowledge, what would you do differently this week than you usually do? List as many things as you can think of. Be sure to consider work, church, family relationships, all your non-Christian friends, and so forth. Be very thorough.

Don't continue until you've given your list of activities some serious thought. Now here's the catch. Can you say for sure that Jesus *won't* return one week from today? Of course not. So why shouldn't you go out and get busy on at least some of the things that you've listed? We need to stop thinking that it would be "nice" if we could be more effective for God and instead allow our spiritual ears to hear a ticking clock. The time is short, and when Jesus *does* come back, He's not going to be giving us a makeup exam to let us look a little better when we are judged for our deeds. If every morning you got up and thought for a moment, *This could be the day,* you would be likely to experience rapid spiritual growth.

Jesus has us on earth to "mind the store," so to speak. We can spend our time and efforts getting whatever we can out of life. Or we can keep in mind that someday the owner is going to return and evaluate us on how we did. If we lead righteous lives, we don't have to be fearful about His return. We can eagerly anticipate it. And perhaps the words that will stand out in eternity more than any others are, "Well done, good and faithful servant!" (Matthew 25:21)

 KEY VERSE:

"God did not appoint us to suffer wrath but to receive salvation through our Lord Jesus Christ. He died for us so that, whether we are awake or asleep, we may live together with Him" (1 Thessalonians 5:9-10).

*Do you ever use spiritual things as an excuse
not to do any real work of value to others?*

9

NO WORK AND
ALL PRAY

(Book of 2 Corinthians)

You may have seen summaries put out by automobile insurance companies of actual statements submitted by people after they have had an accident. Some of their explanations are quite original. Here are a few that were recently run in an Ann Landers column.

"The other car collided with mine without giving warning of its intention."

"I thought my window was down but found it was up when I put my hand through it."

"A pedestrian hit me and went under my car."

"The guy was all over the place. I had to swerve a number of times before I hit him."

"I pulled away from the side of the road, glanced at my mother-in-law, and headed over the embankment."

"The accident occurred when I was attempting to bring my car out of a skid by steering it into the other vehicle."

"I was on my way to the doctor's with rear-end trouble when my universal joint gave way, causing me to have an accident."

"The telephone pole was approaching fast. I was attempting to swerve out of its path when it struck my front end."

"To avoid hitting the bumper of the car in front, I struck the pedestrian."

"My car was legally parked as it backed into the other vehicle."

"An invisible car came out of nowhere, struck my vehicle, and vanished."

"When I saw I could not avoid a collision, I stepped on the gas and crashed into the other car."

"The pedestrian had no idea which direction to go, so I ran him over."

"I saw the slow-moving, sad-faced old gentleman as he bounced off the hood of my car."

"The indirect cause of this accident was a little guy in a small car with a big mouth."

"Coming home, I drove into the wrong house and collided with a tree I don't have."

It's easy to laugh as we read through statements such as these. When people try to dodge the blame for something and word their statements in an attempt to confuse the facts, they sometimes provide a wonderful source of comedy. Yet, at other times, a twisting of the facts isn't funny at all. Whenever people begin to subtly and intentionally distort the truth, you usually need to watch out.

 JOURNEY ONWARD

In the last session you went through Paul's first letter to the Thessalonian church. One of his key points was the certainty of the return of Jesus. And just as it would probably happen today, a lot of people jumped to some wrong conclusions and started their own theories based on what Paul had taught. It didn't take long for some false teachers to influence the Thessalonians by twisting the truth. Some were teaching that the Day of the Lord had already come. Others suggested that since Jesus was going to return, hey, why bother with insignificant things like jobs? Why not just sit around and wait for Him?

Read 2 Thessalonians 1:1-12.
To correct these messed up ways of thinking, a second letter to the Thessalonian church was in order. It was probably less than a year between Paul's two letters. It didn't take long for people back then to start with a perfectly clear teaching and completely distort it into something else. It still doesn't. Bible scholars believe this letter was written from the city of Corinth, based on the fact that three people were together in the same place. These three people were mentioned in Acts 18:5, and now they show up in Paul's salutation. Who were the three traveling companions? (2 Thessalonians 1:1-2)

Even though there were pockets of misguided people within the Thessalonian church, not everyone had been influenced by the false teachers. So Paul didn't "come out shooting" as he began his letter. First he wanted to assure the church people that he had indeed heard some good things about them. What good things were happening there? (1:3)

In what areas did Paul hold up the Thessalonian church as a model for some of the other churches he worked with? (1:4)

Paul reminds his friends in Thessalonica that God is fair. God knows when people suffer on behalf of His kingdom. And what will eventually happen to those who initiate trouble for Christians? (1:5-6)

Getting Personal — *When was the last time you suffered on behalf of God's kingdom?*

Even while we are in the middle of personal distress, God can provide relief. The image Paul gave of the risen Jesus who helps us is quite different than the image we may have of the earthly Jesus. How did Paul describe Jesus to the suffering Thessalonians? (1:7)

Paul affirmed the message of his last letter by reemphasizing that Jesus is going to return. (Here Paul was not referring to the Rapture, but to a later appearance, when Jesus will reward righteousness and punish wickedness.) What's going to happen to people who have refused to believe the Gospel? (1:8-10)

Getting Personal — *Do you know anyone who has refused to believe the Gospel?*

In bold contrast to the "everlasting" judgment of the disobedient people, notice what will be taking place among the Christian community. First, Jesus is going to be "glorified" in His people. Simply put, the fact that we who were once sinners are now "saints" will bring glory to Jesus. And even though we might think we have a pretty complete understanding of the nature of Jesus, when He returns He will be "marveled at among all those who have believed" (1:10).

As he thought about these things, what specific prayers did Paul offer for the Thessalonians? (1:11-12)

Tricky Teachers
Read 2 Thessalonians 2:1-4.

Paul then turned his attention to the specific problems originated by the false teachers in Thessalonica. Not only were these people teaching doctrine that was completely false, but they also used a very tricky method to convince the Thessalonians to believe them. What did these impostors do to try to pass themselves off as genuine authorities to the people in the Thessalonian church? (2:1-2)

Getting Personal — *Have you heard any false teachers who use this same method?*

These false teachers were saying that the Day of the Lord had already come. But Paul made it very clear that a major event would take place before the coming of the Day of the Lord. He describes a man that must first appear. Describe this man (2:3).

What will be this man's mission? (2:4)

Paul reminds the Thessalonians that he had already spoken to them of these things (2:5). But perhaps you know from personal experience how hard it is to keep truth in mind when you get out of a church setting and into the "real" world. For instance, when you hear the Sunday sermon you may become convinced that you need to take a specific action that will help your faith grow (such as witnessing, more commitment to prayer, or whatever). But when you get plugged back into your weekly schedule, sometimes you just don't get around to changing your bad habits. In the case of the Thessalonian church, it wasn't just that they had been separated from Paul. In addition, they were beset by the subtle lies of the false teachers who were *purposely* trying to mislead them. Through his letter, Paul was trying to jog their memory of the truth and get them back on track again.

To be fair to the Thessalonians, we must remember that the church as a whole was undergoing persecution at this time. Paul had specifically mentioned the "persecutions and trials" of the Thessalonian church (1:4). And as the church members looked back into the Old Testament Scriptures, they could read that the "Day of the Lord" would be accompanied by turmoil and calamity. It is somewhat understandable that they could believe some of the things being taught by the false religious leaders. Yet, on the other hand, Paul had just informed them in 1 Thessalonians that Christians could look forward to being "caught up" at the coming of the Lord (1 Thessalonians 4:17). So they should have known better.

The Man of Lawlessness
Read 2 Thessalonians 2:5-16.
Paul continued his discussion of the "man of lawlessness." Based on his description here, this seems to be the Antichrist ("beast") referred to in Revelation 13:11-18. Paul mentioned a force that was holding back the power of this man so that he would only be allowed to act in God's timing. It seems that the Thessalonians knew who (or what) Paul was talking about. But since Paul didn't identify the "one who now holds [lawlessness] back," we can only surmise what Paul was referring to.

Some people have thought that this force might be the Roman Empire, the Jewish people, the work Paul was doing, human governments, Satan, and other things. But according to Paul, the force is supposed to exist until the coming of this "man of lawlessness," and the man will be allowed to vent his power only after the force is removed. Consequently, many people feel that Paul was referring to the power of the Holy Spirit. God's Spirit is certainly strong enough to keep lawlessness in check until the final judgment. As Christians are "caught up" to be with God, the strong influence of the Spirit (through the people of God) will be removed and the man of lawlessness will be free to run rampant.

But what is in the future for the Antichrist—this man of lawlessness? (2 Thessalonians 2:5-8)

How is the lawless one going to persuade people to give him their loyalty? (2:9-10)

Will people be powerless to resist this evil leader, or will it be their choice? Explain your answer (2:10-12).

Getting Personal — *Are you prepared to resist such an evil leader?*

How is it that the Thessalonians were avoiding the trend toward lawlessness? (2:13-15)

What had Jesus' love and grace given Paul? (2:16)

What did Paul say the love and grace of Jesus could do for the Thessalonians? (2:17)

Read 2 Thessalonians 3:1-5.
What did Paul ask the Thessalonians to pray for? (3:1-2)

Getting Personal — *What part does prayer play in protecting you from evil?*

Was Paul having doubts about the future by this time? Explain (3:3-5).

Loafin' Around
Read 2 Thessalonians 3:6-18.
What other problem in the Thessalonian church did Paul address? (3:6)

Paul was as knowledgeable and enthusiastic as anyone about the future return of Jesus. What kind of example was he setting? (3:7-9)

In a Greek society, manual labor was considered work for slaves. "Enlightened" people didn't consider such work appropriate for themselves. And perhaps the "return of Jesus" craze was as good an excuse as any for people to sit around and do nothing. But Paul wouldn't let them off that easily. In his first letter to the Thessalonians, he had instructed the church to "warn those who are idle" (1 Thessalonians 5:14). As he followed up his letter, his previous warning has been upgraded to a "command" (2 Thessalonians 3:6). Pertaining to this issue of laziness, what general rule did Paul give them to live by? (3:10)

Instead of being "busy," what had many of the Thessalonians become? (3:11)

Getting Personal — *How idle are you? Does this reflect anything about your relationship to Christ?*

If you remember your study of the Book of Galatians, you should remember that the Galatian church had similar problems to those here in Thessalonica. And Paul gave similar challenges to the two churches. He told the Galatians: "Let us not become weary in doing good, for at the proper time we will reap a harvest if we do not give up" (Galatians 6:9). What does he tell the Thessalonians? (2 Thessalonians 3:13)

How did Paul suggest that the Thessalonian church enforce the things he had been saying without causing the church to divide into separate "We're Right" and "You're Wrong" groups? (3:14-15)

Paul closed this letter with a prayer for peace — at all times and in every way. In spite of all the turmoil they were facing, Paul made it clear to the Thessalonians that peace was available to them (3:16).

Getting Personal — *Are you experiencing peace? Why or why not?*

Paul also said, "I . . . write this greeting in my own hand" (3:17). You may have noticed similar comments in previous letters. It seems that Paul's usual method of letter writing was to dictate to a secretary. Then at the end, Paul would take the pen and finish the letter himself. This practice became sort of a trademark of Paul's.

 JOURNEY INWARD

If we wanted to be true to the Book of 2 Thessalonians, we should probably do another application section pertaining to the second coming of Jesus. Paul felt that the topic was important enough to write a second letter to the same group of people saying many of the same things (and adding even more new information). And it surely wouldn't hurt to go back, look at the list you made after the last session, and remind yourself of the specific things you need to be doing. (By the way, how well have you done getting started on that list since you finished the last session?) But rather than repeat the exact same topic, we can look at one that is closely related—**the use of time.**

This topic relates closely to the return of Jesus for a couple of reasons. First, since there is only a limited amount of time before Jesus comes back to judge the world, we need to make sure we carve out some time to spend in spiritual development (both for ourselves and the people we know and love). Second, we need to make sure not only that we put in a *quantity* of time doing spiritual things; we also need to make sure it is *quality* time. Some of the Thessalonians were putting in days and weeks waiting for Jesus to return, but they were just sitting around doing nothing while they waited.

First, let's consider the quantity of your time. Think of the past week and estimate how much of your time was spent in each of the following categories. (Use percentages based on your total nonsleeping time to make your estimates.)

You need to put some thought into this, because it's easy to make the figures come out the way you want them to. For instance, if you're at work for eight hours, but have an hour for lunch and sleep through two meetings, you shouldn't count all eight hours toward working. If you watch TV sitcoms for four hours straight and happen to flip past a couple of TV evangelists while changing channels, you can't chalk up those four hours to spiritual development. Be as precise as you can. Put these totals in the first column below.

	QUANTITY OF TIME	QUALITY OF TIME	TOTAL
Time spent in educational development	____%	____%	____%
Time spent in family development	____%	____%	____%
Time spent in physical development	____%	____%	____%
Time spent in spiritual development	____%	____%	____%
Time spent working (Jobs or chores)	____%	____%	____%
Leisure time	____%	____%	____%
Other:_____	____%	____%	____%

Now let's consider the quality of each of the same categories. Go back through the categories and estimate how much of the time is actually productive. For example, perhaps you estimated that 10 percent of all your time is spent in some sort of spiritual development. Now try to figure out how much of that amount is not just "dead time." You may decide that only about a fourth of that time really does you any good. If so, you would put 25 percent in the second column after "Spiritual Development." Do this for each of the categories. (Your leisure time should probably be close to 100 percent.)

Finally, multiply your first and second columns after each of the categories, which will give you the amount of "useful" time in each area. In the above example, you would multiply your 10 percent of time spent in spiritual development by the 25 percent estimate for quality time, and your total for productive spiritual development would be 2.5 percent (.1 x .25).

After you compile all your totals, you should have a pretty good idea where your time is going (or not going). You should also see where your priorities are. (The larger the percentage in the second column, the more worthwhile time you're putting into that activity.) You may also see that you probably aren't "too busy" to do some spiritual things—even with your hectic schedule. You just need to learn to make time for them.

Some of the Thessalonians were "no work and all pray" when it came to the use of their time. (They used "spiritual" things as an excuse not to do any real work of value to others.) Theirs was but one of many serious time problems. So before you conclude this session, spend a few minutes analyzing your chart and thinking of some ways you can get your time divisions closer to the way you *want* them to be. You may need to trim some leisure time or work toward making some of your activities more productive, but it *can* be done with a little determination. And there's no time like . . . oh, you know.

 KEY VERSE:

"May our Lord Jesus Christ Himself and God our Father, who loved us and by His grace gave us eternal encouragement and good hope, encourage your hearts and strengthen you in every good deed and word" (2 Thessalonians 2:16-17).

*Imagine your son, nephew, or neighbor
in charge of your church.*

10

KID STUFF

(Book of 1 Timothy)

You awaken to a beautiful, sunny Saturday. There's nothing you'd rather do today than read the newspaper, do a little yardwork, and attend your son Glenn's Little League baseball game.

As you finish reading the paper, your son bounces in to show you his report on drug testing in the work force that Senator Richards asked him to do. Glenn's 15-step plan was pretty good—even if he did come up with it himself.

With the newspaper read, you move on to trimming the hedges. As you walk out the door, you hear Glenn talking to NASA to see if they have any questions about that new formula he sent them last month. They should have had plenty of time to test it to see if that new superpotent fuel can indeed reduce the weight of booster rockets by 23 percent.

At last it's time for Glenn's game. You've been looking forward all week to getting out and enjoying some sunshine and fresh air. You need it too. Just as it's Glenn's turn to bat, your daughter comes running up. She says, "Glenn has a phone call. It's *him* again."

You don't have to ask who. You get Glenn's attention, pull him from the game, and drive back to the house. Quickly catching your breath, you pick up the phone. "Hello, Mister President," you say. "Sorry to keep you waiting. . . . Glenn is right here."

This call isn't as urgent as some of his are. He doesn't have to send a helicopter for Glenn this time. But he does keep Glenn on the phone for about an hour and a half. And when he finally finishes, Glenn's baseball game is over. As you look through your pocket calendar, you think, *Oh, well. He has another free Saturday in two months. It's just nice that he's needed.*

These kinds of things probably happen all the time to your children or other young people you know. No? Well, if not, why not?

Your answer to this question isn't as trite as you might think. If you respond, "My son or daughter doesn't know anything about all that stuff," that's OK. Lack of expertise is reason enough. But if your answer is, "They're just kids," then you may need to do a lot of reconsidering as you go through this session.

 JOURNEY ONWARD

With this session we begin the "pastoral letters" of Paul. As Paul wrote Timothy (twice) and Titus, he gave these two young men some good information that would help them oversee (or pastor) churches. These letters were written late in Paul's life, and you can tell they are personal and emotional.

As you go through this session and the next, keep in mind that Timothy was a relatively young man. Yet he was one of the people Paul trusted most. Paul had met Timothy early into his second missionary journey, and he took Timothy along with him (Acts 16:1-3). You may have noticed that Paul often commended Timothy to the churches he wrote to, and included Timothy's name in several of his opening salutations.

But when he wrote this letter, Paul and Timothy were separated. Paul was out of his Roman prison and on a fourth missionary journey. He has left Timothy to oversee the church at Ephesus, and he wrote this letter to encourage Timothy. After all, Paul could imagine what kinds of problems a young person could expect as he tried to lead a church where a lot of people were older than the pastor.

How about you? Can you imagine an 18- to 20-year-old being in charge of your church? Try to keep that concept in mind as you go through the next three books of the Bible. You might get a very different perspective on the significance of some of these instructions.

Read 1 Timothy 1:1-20.
It can't be said for sure that Paul was the one who personally helped Timothy discover the truth about the Gospel of Jesus. But Paul had a very close relationship with young Timothy. What did Paul call him? (1 Timothy 1:1-2)

Getting Personal —*Do you have a relationship with a young person similar to Timothy? Do you consider that person a "son" or "daughter"?*

Paul had instructed Timothy to remain in Ephesus and keep a watch out for men who would promote false doctrines. No one knows exactly what the teachings were that used the "myths" and "endless genealogies" that Paul referred to in 1:4. But we are sure of the end result of such teachings: they caused division in the church (1:3-5). Paul's goal, on the other hand, was love. And what three sources of love did Paul mention to Timothy? (1:6-7)

Getting Personal —*Who has been your spiritual mentor?*

Apparently some of these false teachers were attempting to use (or misuse) the Old Testament law. Paul affirmed that the law was good, but he reminded Timothy that the law was directed toward certain kinds of people. For whom was the law written? (1:8-11)

God's grace always stands out in contrast to the law. How had Paul personally benefited from the grace of God? (1:12-14)

It seems that as Paul grew older and more mature, he had a more realistic understanding of himself in relationship to God. He had written to the Corinthians and referred to himself as "the least of the apostles" (1 Corinthians 15:9). A few years later he wrote to the Ephesians and said that he was "less than the least of all God's people" (Ephesians 3:8). Now, as he wrote Timothy even later in his life, how did Paul refer to himself? (1 Timothy 1:15)

Getting Personal — *How would you describe your relationship to God? How does it compare to Paul's relationship with God?*

Paul's opinion of himself wasn't a self-image problem. He clearly saw what he was on a purely human level. But since Paul started out "as low as they come," so to speak, what was he able to proclaim? (1:16-17)

Paul next sounded a little like a boxing trainer. What did he want Timothy to do? (1:18-19)

Paul's image of "shipwrecked" faith is a good one. Sometimes you can be sailing right along in your spiritual development. But if you take your eyes off of Jesus for a little while, you can quickly find yourself off course and in trouble. Such was the case with two people in the Ephesian church whom Paul had been compelled to "hand over to Satan" (to put out of the church for a while, so they would experience "Satan's" world and eventually repent and return to Christian fellowship). The names of these people were Hymenaeus and Alexander (1:20).

Words on Worship
Read 1 Timothy 2:1-15.
Paul instructed Timothy on matters of church functions. What did Paul tell Timothy to do "first of all," and why? (2:1-7)

Getting Personal — *How could you use these verses to structure your prayer life?*

Having just been through the Books of 1 and 2 Thessalonians and seeing that the Day of the Lord is approaching with judgment in store, it's important that you don't miss 1 Timothy 2:3-4. What is God's desire for mankind?

As men lifted up their hands in prayer to God, what attitudes were expected to accompany their action? (2:8)

As women attended church, the way they dressed was very important. What right and wrong methods of dress did Paul list? (2:9-10)

But dress was just the starting point for the women. What other restrictions did the ladies have during a worship service? (2:11-15)

Paul's intended meaning in verse 15 still has Bible scholars stumped. What did he mean by "women will be saved through childbearing"? Some people suggest Paul meant that women would be kept safe through the process of childbirth if they maintained the godly qualities that he had listed. Some say that this is a reference to the human birth of Jesus that made salvation possible in the first place. Others think that since women seemed to have so many restrictions in *public* worship, they would be saved from insignificance through their roles as wives and mothers. (Remember that the first century didn't offer women nearly as much opportunity as this century does.) But even though part of this reference is obscure, the rest is very clear: women are to "continue in faith, love and holiness with propriety."

Elders and Deacons
Read 1 Timothy 3:1-16.
Now before you start thinking that those poor women had so many nitpicky things to concern themselves with in the church, move ahead to see what Paul said about the men who would be running the church. What kind of character was required of an overseer? (3:1-5)

These overseers could be young, as Timothy was, but they weren't to be recent converts to Christianity. Why not? (3:6-7)

The expectations of deacons weren't much different than those of pastors. What did it take for a man to become a deacon? (3:8-13)

All of these instructions were important to Paul, who feared that he might be delayed from returning to Ephesus. Paul wrote this letter to Timothy for the primary purpose of sharing these procedures. Proper church conduct is especially important when we remember that the church is the body of Christ. What six things about Jesus should we keep in mind as we adopt these worship habits? (3:14-16)

Read 1 Timothy 4:1-16.
It is essential to review what we know for sure about Jesus when false teachers hit us with doctrines that don't ring true. What should God's people keep in mind when confronted by such false teachers? (4:1-5)

Getting Personal — *What false teachings have you heard most recently?*

We need to train ourselves to know what to do in such situations. Paul said that a physical workout might do some good, but what can you do that has even more value? (4:6-10)

What other things did Paul emphasize to his young friend? (4:11-16)

Getting Personal — *If you had been Timothy as you received these instructions, how do you think you would have responded? Be specific.*

Read 1 Timothy 5:1-25.
What kinds of relationships should Christians have? (5:1-2)

One of the big issues at this time was the care of widows. Perhaps you remember from the Book of Acts that this was one of the first problems to arise after the formation of the church (Acts 6:1). So Paul gave some detailed instructions on this matter. Were all the widows to receive equal treatment? Explain (1 Timothy 5:3-8).

Apparently the churches kept lists of widows whom they should take care of. How could a widow get on this list? (5:9-10)

Why was there an age requirement? (5:11-15)

In what cases would widows who qualified for church help not receive it? Why? (5:16)

Getting Personal—*Can you think of any widows/widowers to whom you could minister?*

Why did Paul say that certain elders deserved double honor? (5:17)

Apparently Paul wasn't just talking about pats on the back either. He saw the functions of running a church—especially preaching and teaching—to be worth some monetary compensation. What two scriptural principles does he quote to support his statement? (5:18)

In addition to money, elders deserve respect from church members. What was one safeguard to prevent an elder's reputation from being ruined by mistake or by one person's personal grudge? (5:19-20)

Paul made it clear that he wasn't just spouting off his opinion on these matters; he spoke for God (5:21). He didn't want Timothy to be too quick to ordain someone as an elder. He *did* want Timothy to keep himself pure (5:22).

But perhaps Timothy was trying to be too pure. He had apparently decided that he wouldn't drink alcoholic beverages. Yet he had frequent illnesses, and the water quality at this time was often far from healthful levels. So what did Paul suggest to Timothy? (5:23)

Getting Personal—*What are your views on the use of alcohol?*

In what way did Paul say good deeds are like bad deeds? (5:24-25)

Read 1 Timothy 6:1-21.
How should Christian slaves behave? (6:1-2)

What is the connection between godliness and financial gain? Explain (6:3-10).

Paul again challenged Timothy to "fight the good fight of the faith" by pursuing Christlike qualities and avoiding evil. How long was Timothy supposed to do this? (6:11-16)

Paul had just addressed the problem of people without money who wanted it. Now he referred to people who already have lots of money. What attitude should they have? Why? (6:17-19)

Getting Personal — *What kinds of attitudes do you have toward money?*

And after one final challenge to his young friend (6:20-21), Paul signed off. He will have more to say to Timothy in his next letter (and your next session), but we have plenty to think about so far.

 JOURNEY INWARD

Maybe you usually resist having a young person tell you what to do. But it's obvious from Paul's letter that he had a great deal of respect for Timothy. Paul knew the pressures a young person would have trying to perform the huge task of overseeing a church. His purpose in writing was to help Timothy keep his spirits up so he wouldn't fail in the massive responsibility he had been given. So from this letter, you should discover the value of **mentoring young people.**

Are young people an essential part of your church? If they stopped attending, how long would it take most of the adults to notice? Are you being influenced by any young people in your church? Are you influencing them?

Adults are notoriously slow to recognize the abilities of young people. So let's go through some of the challenges that Paul gave to Timothy and see how you are stacking up as a mentor.

(1) 1 Timothy 2:9-10—What kind of example do you provide for other church members in regard to dress and appearance? Do you ever give them an opportunity to complain about you? Or do you dress "modestly, with decency and propriety . . . with good deeds"?

(2) 1 Timothy 3:15—How would young people in your church evaluate your ability to "know how you ought to conduct yourself in God's household"? Are you an example of humility, alertness, and spiritual maturity?

(3) 1 Timothy 4:12—What kind of example do you set in each of the following areas:

❑ In speech? (Think of what you say directly to others as well as what they might overhear you telling people your own age.)

❑ In life? (What if they saw you at home, at work, with friends after work, etc.?)

❑ In love? (Consider your marital or family relationships. How much love do you show the young people in your church and community?)

❑ In faith? (How's your spiritual development coming along, as far as they can tell?)

❑ In purity? (Can you be honest with young people, or do you feel the need to be hypocritical and keep a lot of stuff hidden?)

(4) 1 Timothy 5:8—How are you doing in providing for your family members? They may not need lots of your cash to get by, but maybe they're "needy" when it comes to receiving love and respect from you. What are some things that you should be "providing" for them that you aren't yet doing?

As you review your answers to the previous questions, you should be coming up with a list of things you need to be doing. Keep in mind that one of your goals should be to treat young men as brothers and young women as sisters—with absolute purity (5:1-2).

When you start coming through by showing maturity and respect for the young people in your church, perhaps they will begin to treat you more like a leader. This won't happen overnight, or even during the first month or so. If you have been exhibiting an attitude that young people are insignificant and have little to contribute to the body of Christ, it may take you a long time to build appropriate relationships with those young observers. Timothy stood out as a leader at Ephesus because of his long-term commitment to God and his devotion to his responsibilities at the church. There's no reason why you can't assume Paul's role and encourage young people in your church and community to be committed and devoted to the work of the church.

Running a church isn't just for old people—it's kids' stuff too. Your young people are going to be the church of tomorrow, and you need to get started mentoring them today.

 KEY VERSE:

"Don't let anyone look down on you because you are young, but set an example for the believers in speech, in life, in love, in faith and in purity" (1 Timothy 4:12).

*When it comes to sharing the Gospel,
shyness is no excuse.*

11

SHYING AWAY
FROM SHYNESS

(Book of 2 Timothy)

M onday, 3:08 P.M.
Grant is participating in the most important meeting of his career. The topic is, "Desktop Publishing: Should SC Industries Purchase an Apple Computer?" He has the unenviable job of defending the purchase. But Grant has facts and statistics to support everything he says, and as the meeting ends, Grant's request is approved. Grant tells one of his friends, "It's amazing how you can take an unpopular request and convince people to see it your way—if you're prepared, that is."

Tuesday, 7:48 P.M.
Marcie is just about finished scouring her neighborhood to find new people to sign her "Save the Animals" petition. It is a cause she believes in, so she has no trouble going up to perfect strangers and asking for their signatures and contributions. Her charming manner convinces a lot of people to sign.

Wednesday, 4:28 P.M.
Jack gathers his courage in the lobby of the Farnsworth Industrial Headquarters building. He has outgrown his job at the fast-food chain, and is looking for a business internship that will challenge him as he finishes his last year of college. He is determined to let his potential employer see the best side of him. As he is called into the office to be interviewed, he begins with a firm handshake and ends with a "Thank you very much for your time. I'm sure you won't be disappointed if you decide to offer me this job."

Friday, 11:00 A.M.
Millie's family sits around the TV set to watch Millie and three other people

on *Win, Sketch, or Lose*. As captain, Millie has to draw clues for the bonus questions. She was a little nervous at first, with the knowledge that all eyes were on her. But she quickly settles down because of the importance of her responsibility. As she begins to relax, she finds that she can think clearer and sketch more quickly. Thanks to her coolness under pressure, her team squeaks by the team that won it all last year. A win next week will move them into the championship.

Sunday, 10:15 A.M.
Grant, Marcie, Jack, and Millie sit in Sunday School class, listening to what the teacher has to say about sharing their faith with others. It is obvious that none of them agree with him. And as soon as he opens the subject up for discussion, they all have something to say.

GRANT: I sense a lot of resistance from people about Christianity. And as soon as they make some kind of objection, I have no idea what to say. So why bother?

MARCIE: Yeah, and I just don't feel right interfering with someone else's privacy. People have the right to be left alone.

JACK: It's just too intimidating to approach perfect strangers and open up your life. If people want to know about Christianity, why don't they go to church and talk to the pastor?

MILLIE: Sharing your faith with strangers really puts you on the spot. It takes a certain kind of personality to be that bold. And I think we're all just too shy to do it.

What do you think? Do you believe that these people are really shy? Or do you think shyness is something they use as an excuse? Do you know anyone who uses shyness as an excuse to get out of trying to tell others about Jesus?

We aren't excused from Christian responsibility just because we want to pass ourselves off as shy people. We all seem to do what we need to do when the cause is important enough to us. We find the courage to meet strangers, anticipate their questions, travel into unfamiliar territory, and so forth. We will do the same thing for God when our relationship with Him becomes important enough to us.

That's not to say that some people aren't truly shy. Some are very, very timid. But when it comes to the importance of sharing the Gospel, no one is excused. God will definitely help people with their shyness and provide courage to help them through any situation. God's antidote to shyness will be discussed in this session.

 JOURNEY ONWARD

In the last session you got to know Timothy a little better through Paul's comments to him. You saw how his youth didn't stand in the way of his importance to the church. In this session you will see that Timothy was not only young, but more than likely he was also a shy person. The advice Paul sends to "Timid Timothy" in this letter can help you with your own shyness.

This was probably Paul's last letter, and he wrote from a Roman dungeon (during Nero's reign). He had been released from his previous imprisonment when he lived in his own rented house (Acts 28:30). This time the conditions were much worse, to the point where his friends even had a hard time finding out where he was being kept. And according to tradition, Paul was beheaded shortly after he wrote this letter.

Read 2 Timothy 1:1-18.
But even as the cloud of death seems to be hovering over Paul's head, what was he thinking about as he opened his second letter to Timothy? (2 Timothy 1:1-2)

What wish did Paul express to Timothy? (1:3-4)

Timothy's father was a Gentile, but his mother was Jewish (Acts 16:1). What kind of faith did Timothy have as a youngster? Explain (2 Timothy 1:5).

Timothy had grown into a spiritually equipped man of God. What did Paul want him to do with the "spark" of a gift he had received? (1:6)

Sometimes people who don't know better think of Christians as wimpy, meek, washed-out personalities with no backbones. But Paul was insistent that God doesn't give us the spirit of timidity. Instead, what kind of spirit *does* God provide for us? (1:7)

What things did Paul say that "Timid Timothy" could do after he received God's power to get over his shyness? (1:8-11)

How did Paul keep from being timid (or ashamed)? (1:12)

Paul again challenged Timothy to remain faithful to his calling (1:13-14). Paul's concern was understandable because he recalled some of the personal consequences he was currently experiencing as the result of a lack of faithfulness. How was Paul suffering because of the lack of faithfulness of other Christians? (1:15)

Perhaps it wasn't exactly a lack of faithfulness that caused these people to desert Paul in a time of need. Maybe Paul's friends were just "shy" and didn't want to be seen by Roman soldiers who reported to the Emperor Nero. But either way, Paul was left alone in a time when he really could have used some friends. And in times like that, the few people who do come through for you seem very special. For example, the name Onesiphorus is way down on the list of recognizable biblical names. But this man was singled out by Paul. Why? (1:16-18)

Read 2 Timothy 2:1-13.
Yet it takes more than one faithful person to be sure the Gospel continues to spread. How did Paul instruct Timothy to see that the Gospel keeps spreading? (2:1-2)

Paul then related what he was saying about faithfulness to three different areas of life that most people could relate to. Review 2 Timothy 2:3-7 and explain how the following professions require faithfulness. (Use your common sense as well as what Paul refers to in his letter.)

❑ Soldiers

❑ Athletes

❑ Farmers

Getting Personal — *What do you have in common with these three professions?*

Even though Paul was chained, what thoughts gave him confidence? (2:8-13)

Quit the Quarreling
Read 2 Timothy 2:14-26.

Paul reminded Timothy that it's easy to get involved with bickering and quarreling that doesn't do anyone any good. Rather than misusing his words, what did Paul challenge Timothy to do? (2:14-16)

What example did Paul give to demonstrate how ignorant talk could be destructive? (2:17-18)

Getting Personal — *How would you rate yourself in regard to meaningless, destructive talk?*

Who suffers more from the meaningless talk that Paul has described: the church or the people doing the talking? Explain (2:19).

Paul compared people to dishes in a house. He said that most households have different qualities of dishware. If you're at home by yourself, you may microwave some pizza, slop it down on a paper plate, and toss the plate out when you're finished. But when you have a date or some guests that you feel are important, you use the good dishes, clean them up, and return them to the shelf for the next special occasion. Paul's suggestion was that Christians shouldn't be paper plates. We should always strive to be people of quality, available for Jesus to use (and reuse) whenever He needs us (2:20-21). What are some practical ways we can prepare ourselves for God's service? (2:22-24)

We shouldn't be so shy that we don't accomplish anything for God, but we aren't supposed to go pushing people around, either. What's the proper way to handle opposition? (2:25-26)

Read 2 Timothy 3:1-13.
But no matter how hard we properly try to convince people to obey God, we will never win them all. Paul gave Timothy a list of people's attitudes that would be present as the time of Jesus' return gets close. Read through his list, and write down any attitudes you see that are common among people today (3:1-7).

Getting Personal — *Are you guilty of any of these attitudes?*

Paul named two men who opposed Moses who aren't named elsewhere in the Bible—Jannes and Jambres. According to Jewish tradition, these were Pharaoh's magicians who stood against Moses when he first tried to get the Egyptian leader's permission to free the Israelites (Exodus 7). Why don't people like these two ever succeed in the long run? (2 Timothy 3:8-9)

What is in store for people who lead godly lives? (3:10-13)

God's Breath
Read 2 Timothy 3:14-17.
In what four specific ways will God's Word help Christians? (3:14-17)

Read 2 Timothy 4:1-22.
Again, as he did frequently, Paul made sure his readers know that he wasn't just expressing one man's opinion. He wanted no room for doubt that he was speaking for God. So in the presence of God and Jesus, what challenge did Paul put before Timothy? (4:1-2)

Why was Timothy's work going to be so important? (4:3-5)

As he had done in his letter to the Philippians, Paul referred to himself as "being poured out like a drink offering" (Philippians 2:17; 2 Timothy 4:6). At this point in his life, Paul had been working about 30 years in the role of an apostle. And he knew that his death wasn't far off. Thinking back over his life, Paul was able to confidently make an amazing statement. Of what was he convinced? (2 Timothy 4:7)

What was Paul looking forward to? (4:8)

But you should know Paul well enough by now to know that he wasn't about to roll over and play dead. Not even in a grimy Roman dungeon. Not even with a sentence of the Roman Empire hanging over his head. Not even when he was feeling incredibly lonely. Even in these circumstances he was busy making plans. For one thing, Paul desperately wanted to see Timothy. One of Paul's associates, named Demas, had been in Rome with Paul. He had previously been mentioned as a coworker in the ministry (Colossians 4:14). But Demas had suddenly deserted Paul. Why? (2 Timothy 4:9-10)

Getting Personal — *Is there anyone you desperately need to see or talk with right now? Why?*

Others of Paul's friends had left to minister elsewhere (4:11-12). Luke was still with Paul at this time, but Paul really wanted to see Timothy. And Paul asked Timothy to bring Mark with him when he came. Don't forget that John Mark was the one whom Paul had previously refused to take on his second missionary journey (Acts 15:36-41). Apparently, regardless of whatever had caused his earlier hesitation, Mark had redeemed himself in Paul's eyes. (Most of us can be thankful that God gives us second chances and doesn't give up on us when we make our first mistake — or our second — or our 500th.)

What did Paul ask Timothy to bring when he came? (2 Timothy 4:12-13)

Paul had been harmed in some way by a person named Alexander. And though he wasn't holding a personal grudge against this man, neither was he completely ignoring Alexander's offense. Why not? (4:14-15)

You may remember from your history books that there was a large fire in Rome in A.D. 64 while Nero was emperor. Nero blamed it on the Christians, and intense persecution followed. Paul's second letter to Timothy was written in A.D. 67. While some of the intensity of the harsh feelings toward Christians may have died down, it's not surprising that Paul was losing some of his regular supporters. After being previously deserted by everyone, how did Paul feel as he concluded his letter? (4:16-18)

Paul's final comments (4:19-22) were personal greetings to his friends as well as one last request for Timothy to arrive before winter (which may explain why he was asking for his cloak). From a chronological viewpoint, this is the last we hear of Paul. But the next session will cover two more of his previously written letters, and we'll get to know some more of Paul's friends a little better.

 ## JOURNEY INWARD

As we reflect on what Paul had to say in 2 Timothy, we want to take a close look at **shyness.** It would be incorrect to say that shyness is wrong in all circumstances. It's certainly more preferable to be a little reserved than to be a loudmouth who offends everyone you meet. Nobody likes to put up with a wise guy all the time. But if your shyness prevents others from seeing the real you (and possibly the presence of Jesus in your life), then you need to start opening up a bit more.

For each of the following situations, circle the symbol that best reflects your level of shyness. Then following each situation, come up with some ways that you can be a little bolder when you need to be.

How shy are you when it comes to:

Meeting new people?
How can you become bolder?

Speaking to groups?
How can you become bolder?

Handling conflict?
How can you become bolder?

Relating to others?
How can you become bolder?

Receiving compliments?
How can you become bolder?

Sharing the Gospel?
How can you become bolder?

The way you feel about yourself?
How can you become bolder?

It's important in all of these areas to remember that boldness doesn't mean showing off, smarting off, being boastful, raising your voice, or anything of the sort. Paul warned Timothy about being too timid, but he also kept reminding him to be gentle, patient, and loving. So we must find the proper level between shyness and shallowness, timidity and terror, boldness and bellowing. But if we remember that it is God who provides the power, love, and self-discipline (or as some Bible versions translate it, "a sound mind"), we shouldn't exceed the boundaries of good taste. We'll learn not to be so afraid of being ourselves, saying what we think, and telling others about the God that we serve. It's worth overcoming our shyness to have that level of confidence in our lives. Try it and see.

 KEY VERSE:
"God did not give us a spirit of timidity, but a spirit of power, of love and of self-discipline" (2 Timothy 1:7).

*Wouldn't the world be a better place if people
didn't hold grudges for things that happen accidentally?*

12

GIVE THEM A PEACE
OF YOUR MIND

(Books of Titus and Philemon)

You and a friend are out for a bicycle ride through the park on a gorgeous summer day. You're taking it pretty easy and soaking in the sights. Mildly aware of the little old lady jogging up ahead, you jokingly make a note not to run over her. But wouldn't you know it? Just as you get up to where she is, a motorcycle roars past you (illegally) going the other way. The lady apparently heard the noise of the motor above the music on her Walkman, and she stopped to turn and look. You and your friend were looking behind you too, and before you turned back around, you ran right over the lady's foot.

She was very gracious, and wouldn't have minded at all, except for that large painful corn on her big toe. But she thought she would just hobble down to the nearby lake to soak her foot in some water for a moment. She said she's OK and that you can go. Your friend is ready to flee the scene of the crime before having to leave names and addresses behind, but you can't go off and leave this poor lady with no one to tend to her if she needs help.

You follow her down to the water and ask, "Are you sure you're all right?" She apparently didn't hear you, so you ask again (a little louder). Still no response. Finally you get right behind her and yell, "ARE YOU SURE YOU'RE OK?" She whirls around quickly with a look of surprise and terror in her eyes. She must be so scared that she forgot her foot was hurt. As she puts her weight on it, she immediately topples backward into the water like one of those trees you see in the lumberjack movies.

You jump right in to save her, and you instantly: (1) Rip the new jogging jacket her five-year-old granddaughter had just given her, (2) Lose her glasses in the lake, (3) Ruin her Walkman, not to mention the cassette (Who would have figured her for a Neil Young fan?), and (4) Drag her sore foot across the rocks and sand as you pull her out of the water. Other than that, she was fine (except for a 30-minute coughing/gurgling fit).

By the time she's finally able to speak, a large crowd and a large policeman have gathered. (Funny, but you don't seem to see your friend among the people in the crowd.) The lady explains to the policeman that in her clumsiness she stumbled into the water and you heroically pulled her out. But judging from the expression on the policeman's face, you have a sneaking suspicion that he may have seen what actually happened.

After the crowd dissipates, all you can do is keep stammering, "I'm sorry. I'm so, so sorry. I'm so very sorry." Frankly, you're expecting the usual response of, "You'll be hearing from my lawyer." But the lady tells you, "Listen, Dear. Don't worry. These things happen. My foot isn't seriously injured, and all these other things can be replaced. Life is too short for holding grudges. Go on now, and have fun." And as she limps off into the distance, you have learned a valuable lesson. (You will never, ever go back into that park again!)

Wouldn't the world be a better place if people didn't hold grudges for things that happen accidentally? And if people were less hasty to point fingers when things go wrong? And if you didn't have to worry about lawsuits every time you looked at someone the wrong way?

We all need to be accountable for our actions. But it's a fact that we live in an imperfect world. We're going to make mistakes. We're going to let people down sometimes. We're going to have people do the same to us.

The way we handle those situations tells others a lot about us. And if we call ourselves *Christian*, the way we handle those situations will also influence the way others think about the *Christ* part of that title. Issues such as forgiveness, restitution, peacemaking, and so forth cannot be taken lightly in a world such as ours.

JOURNEY ONWARD

In this session, we aren't going to look at one of Paul's letters—we're going to look at *two*. (Don't worry. They're both short.) The first is another of Paul's pastoral letters. You've already been through the two pastoral letters addressed to Timothy; this third and final one is written to Titus. You've probably noticed Titus' name turning up throughout Paul's previous letters. In this session, you finally get a closer look at this guy.

Keep in mind that Titus was a Gentile convert whom Paul had taken along on some of his travels. He was also the person whom Paul took before the church council to determine whether or not circumcision was necessary for all Christians as it had been for all Jews. At this time, while Timothy was overseeing the church in Ephesus, Titus was pastor of the church in Crete (the fourth largest island in the Mediterranean Sea). Titus' job probably wasn't one all of us would enjoy. As you will soon see, the people of Crete weren't exactly honorable.

Read Titus 1:1-4.
The introduction to Paul's letter to Titus is more complex than most of his previous ones have been. And you shouldn't be tempted to whip through it to get to the real "message" of the letter. This salutation is jam-packed with terrific information about God. List everything Paul tells us about God.

(NOTE: "God's elect" is a way of saying people whom God has specially chosen. Or more simply, "Christians.")

Paul was a Jew from birth and Titus was a Gentile. What kind of relationship did these two men have, and what made their relationship possible? (Titus 1:4)

151

The Churches in Crete
Read Titus 1:5-16.
We don't know much about Paul's previous visit to Crete. The Book of Acts records no such visit of Paul and Titus, so we can assume that it was after Paul's release from his two-year term in Rome. Apparently Paul wasn't able to stay long in Crete, so what did he want Titus to do? (1:5)

As he had done with Timothy, Paul provided Titus with a list of qualifications to look for as elders were selected for the Cretan churches. You read through most of these same qualifications when you went through 1 Timothy. Once again, what qualities are required of a church elder? (1:6-9)

Why was Titus told to be so selective as he looked for people to oversee the church? (1:10)

Getting Personal — *Have you ever served on a search or nominating committee for church officers? How selective were you?*

What motivated the false teachers in Crete, and what was the result of their teaching? (1:11)

Even the people who lived in Crete had a rather low opinion of their fellow islanders. What was the proverb that one of the Cretan authors had written about his people? (1:12)

Crete may not sound like the place you would choose to take a vacation, but it was a location desperately in need of a godly church. So what was Paul's instruction to Titus in regard to handling the people of Crete? (1:13-14)

What does a corrupt lifestyle do to the development of a person's faith? (1:15-16)

Read Titus 2:1-15.
Titus was in a position similar to Timothy's. He was young in relation to many of the other church members. So what advice did Paul give Titus for handling each of the following groups of people within the church:

❑ Older men (2:1-2)

❑ Older women (2:3)

❑ Younger women (2:4-5)

❑ Younger men (2:6-7)

❑ People who opposed Titus (2:7-8)

❑ Slaves (2:9-10)

Notice that Paul told Titus to "teach" most of these groups. But when he got around to the "younger men" segment of the church, Paul told Titus to "set them an example." Since Titus was a young man himself, he wasn't just supposed to *tell* others his own age what to do. He was supposed to *show* them.

Why should all these groups of people in the church be willing to do as Titus instructed them? (2:11)

Why is it so important to try to lead godly lives on a daily basis? (2:12-14)

What was Titus to do after teaching the people in Crete? (2:15)

Read Titus 3:1-15.
Keeping in mind that many of the Cretans were "liars, evil brutes [and] lazy gluttons" (1:12), many of the basic teachings of Christianity must have seemed foreign to them. What "new" ways of living did Paul tell Titus to pass along to the people of Crete? (3:1-2)

But neither Paul nor Titus were looking down their noses at the Cretans. How did Paul describe his own past and the past of most other Christians? (3:3)

How does a relationship with Jesus change a person's perspective on life? (3:4-7)

Getting Personal — *Of the ingredients listed in verses 4-7, which one is key to your salvation? Why?*

Titus was instructed to stress the truths of Christianity (3:8) and avoid other senseless teachings that would split the church members (3:9). How was Titus to handle divisive people? (3:10-11)

Paul promised to send someone else to Crete so Titus could rejoin Paul at Nicopolis for the winter. What last thing did Paul reemphasize that Christian people need to learn to do? (3:12-15)

Philemon
Read Philemon 1-25.
At this point we leave Paul's letter to Titus behind and move ahead to his letter to Philemon. This letter is different from most of Paul's others. It's the shortest, for one thing. It wasn't addressed to a church or someone in a pastoral capacity. Rather, the letter to Philemon is a personal appeal to a

man in the church at Colosse. Based on Paul's opening, what kind of person do you think Philemon was? (Philemon 1-3)

Paul immediately referred to several of Philemon's positive qualities. For what reasons did Paul praise Philemon? (4-7)

And after his tactful lead-in, Paul got around to the reason for his letter. He wanted a favor from Philemon. Paul suggested that in his role as an apostle, he could "order" Philemon to honor his request. But instead, Paul made his appeal based on love. What did Paul want Philemon to do? (8-11)

It seems that Philemon had a slave named Onesimus. (The name *Onesimus* meant "useful.") Apparently Onesimus had run away from Philemon, probably after stealing something from him. But while "on the lam," Onesimus had come into contact with Paul and had become a Christian. So Paul used a clever play on words. He suggested to Philemon that his slave, Onesimus ("useful"), had become "useless." But after becoming a Christian, he was "useful" again. And not only had Onesimus become useful to Philemon, but he was also useful to Paul (and the church) as well.

Getting Personal — *Do you have a nickname? Does it reflect anything about your character?*

What was Paul's first idea as to how Onesimus could again live up to his "useful" name? (12-13)

Why didn't Paul do what he felt like doing? (14)

When Paul asked Philemon to take back Onesimus, it was no small favor he was asking. In this culture, slave owners were within the law to put captured runaway slaves to *death*. Paul wasn't just asking Philemon to let Onesimus live. He wanted him to treat Onesimus as a Christian brother. Paul even suggested that Onesimus may have been separated from Philemon for a reason. What reason did he think may have been behind Onesimus' escape? (15-16)

Paul then appealed to Philemon as a personal friend to grant him this favor. What other things did he say to convince Philemon to again look on Onesimus with good favor? (17-19)

Did Paul believe that Philemon would do as he had asked? (20-21)

Paul was in prison as he wrote this letter. He made a request for himself in addition to what he had asked on Onesimus' behalf. What did Paul ask of Philemon? (1:22)

And as Paul concluded his note to Philemon, the section of the Bible we know as the "Pauline Epistles" ends. From this point onward, the New Testament contains the writings of other people. But before you move on to meet some of those new authors, pause for a moment to apply what you've seen here in Titus and Philemon.

JOURNEY INWARD

Actually, Titus and Philemon are quite different in content and purpose. When writing Titus, Paul was concerned about church business and the importance of godliness in contrast to the rampant unrighteousness in Crete. On the other hand, Philemon is a very personal letter with Paul coming across more like a father figure than a church leader. But the two letters have a common theme, even though that theme is developed in different ways. Let's see what these two books can tell us about **forgiveness.**

The theme of forgiveness is more subtle in Titus than in Philemon. But everything Paul had to say about the business of the church was based on the simple fact that Jesus has forgiven us. Paul's basic instructions to Titus were to tell those lazy Cretans that all Christians started out in a state of sin and depravity. But because we have responded to the forgiveness God offers through the death of His Son, we have become heirs of God who look forward to eternal life. So the issue of forgiveness is key to the order and organization of the church.

Then as we move on to Paul's letter to Philemon, we see a different application of the importance of forgiveness. Because God has forgiven *us*, we are expected to forgive *one another* in the same way. As Christians, we cannot take the free gift of forgiveness that Jesus offers, and then tell other people to go jump whenever they offend us. The gift of forgiveness, once received, is then to be the model for our actions from that point on.

Another point that should be noted is the importance of third parties to act as peacemakers. When some people tend to overlook the need for forgiveness, others of us need to gently prod the grudge-holders into resolving their conflict situations. Even though Onesimus was repentant, Philemon would have been within his rights to unload with both barrels if his slave ever showed up again. But Paul was ready and eager to mediate between the two parties. We should look for opportunities where we can do the same.

The most important element of forgiveness, naturally, is what God does for us. But other sessions have focused on responding to the love and forgiveness of God. So as we end this session, let's put more of our emphasis on forgiving each other.

Give Them a Peace of Your Mind

For each of the following situations, check the level of forgiveness that would best describe your reaction in that situation.

	No Need to Forgive	Would Gladly Forgive	Would Reluctantly Forgive	Would Never Forgive
Someone interrupts your lunch, thinking you're a famous movie star.				
Someone interrupts your lunch, thinking you're an escaped mental patient.				
Someone says you've been looking a little thinner these days.				
Someone says you seem to have put on a few pounds lately.				
Your baby daughter spills cranberry juice all over your 25-page report.				
Some jerk at work spills cranberry juice all over your 25-page report.				
Your spouse is an hour late picking you up.				
The person you commute to work with is 15 minutes late picking you up.				
Your close friends have a party and forget to invite you.				
Your not-so-close friends have a party and forget to invite you.				

As you look back at the responses you marked, you may discover that perhaps your willingness to forgive is based more on relationships than on the actual offenses. We're quick to forgive some people for the same action for which we condemn others. That's one area where most of us need to be better imitators of God's forgiveness. If we only forgive certain people, we don't reflect the same kind of forgiveness that we've received. (What if God had decided to compare you to everyone else before deciding whether or not you should be forgiven for your sins?)

So think of all the people whom you are holding grudges against. List those people and their specific offenses in the space below. (And use extra paper if you need it.)

Now think of people whom *you* have offended (whether intentionally or not). Even if you only suspect that certain people have something against you, include them on the list. Be as precise as you can.

The next step is to spend some time in serious prayer. True forgiveness never comes easily. (God's forgiveness cost Jesus His life.) So request some supernatural help. For each of the situations that you mentioned on your first list, ask God for a spirit of genuine forgiveness. Then go to those people while they're on your mind and straighten out whatever the problem is. Don't just *say* that they are forgiven; *show* them as well.

Also pray for the situations on your second list. Go to those people as well, and ask them to forgive whatever you've done. Even if you're not sure whether they're upset at you or not, assume that they are. That way you can see if anything is standing in the way of a strong friendship. (Of course, you can't force them to forgive you if they don't *want* to, but at least you will have done everything possible to settle accounts with them.)

Forgiveness is one of the key ingredients to making sure your faith functions correctly. When forgiveness isn't being showered in abundance throughout your relationships, you're going to encounter problems. So if you can't work things out with someone no matter how hard you try, look for a third party who will "go to bat" for you with the other person. Also look for conflicts where *you* can act as a middle person. Don't let any problems exist where you can get rid of them instead. Do everything within your power to continually practice forgiveness. Without forgiveness, there is no peace of mind. And without peace of mind, there can be no peace within relationships.

Until people can realize that all is forgiven, they won't be able to turn their attention to other important matters of faith. And until you personally begin to forgive those who "offend" you, you're probably not going to sense God's closeness in your life. Without forgiveness, you lose, other people lose, and Christianity as a whole suffers. When you learn to forgive, *everybody* wins. Now that you know what to do, all that's left is to just *do* it.

 KEY VERSE:
"The grace of God that brings salvation has appeared to all men. It teaches us to say "No" to ungodliness and worldly passions, and to live self-controlled, upright and godly lives in this present age, while we wait for the blessed hope — the glorious appearing of our great God and Savior, Jesus Christ" (Titus 2:11-13).

BEFORE YOU LEAVE

We hope you'll "forgive" this final request. Could you please take a couple of minutes and fill out the survey on the next page? We value your input on our products as we try to target our materials for your specific needs. Please let us know what you think.

We also encourage you to continue through the next book of the **BibleLog for Adults Series:** *Home At Last* (Book 4). It is the last book in the New Testament series and will cover the section of the Bible from Hebrews through Revelation. As you know, that section contains some bold passages and revealing insights into what's in store for God's people. If you've come this far, it would be a shame not to continue through to the "happy ending" of the Bible. Thanks for your interest so far, and may God continue to reward you as you experience His Word on a regular basis. Enjoy the rest of your trip!

GETTING TOGETHER

A Leader's Guide for Small Groups

Before you jump into this leader's guide in all the excitement of preparing for Session 1, take time to read these introductory pages.

Because the basic Bible content of the study is covered inductively in 12 chapters, group members should work through each assigned chapter before attending the small group meeting. This isn't always easy for busy adults, so encourage group members with a phone call or note between some of the meetings. Help them manage their time by pointing out how they can cover a few pages in a few minutes daily, and having them identify a regular time that they can devote to the **BibleLog** study.

Notice that each session is structured to include the following:

- ❏ Session Topic—a brief statement of purpose for the session.
- ❏ Icebreaker—an activity to help group members get better acquainted with the session topic and/or each other.
- ❏ Discussion Questions—a list of questions to encourage group participation.
- ❏ Optional Activities—supplemental ideas that will enhance your study.
- ❏ Assignment—directions for preparation and suggestions for memorization of key Scriptures.

Here are a few tips that can lead to more effective small group studies:

- ❏ Pray for each group member, asking the Lord to help you create an open atmosphere, so that everyone will feel free to share with each other and you.
- ❏ Encourage group members to bring their Bibles to each session. This series is based on the *New International Version*, but it is good to have several translations on hand for purposes of comparison.
- ❏ Start on time. This is especially important for the first meeting because it will set the pattern for the rest of the course.

❑ Begin with prayer, asking the Holy Spirit to open hearts and minds and to give understanding so that Truth will be applied.

❑ Involve everyone. As learners, we retain only 10 percent of what we hear, 20 percent of what we see, 65 percent of what we hear and see, *but* 90 percent of what we hear, see, and do.

❑ Promote a relaxed environment. Arrange your chairs in a circle or semi-circle. This promotes eye contact among members and encourages more dynamic discussion. Be relaxed in your own attitude and manner.

1

Session Topic: Through our vulnerability, others are able to see the God whom we serve.

Icebreakers

Divide into pairs and find out as much as possible about your partner. Then sit back to back and answer the following questions: **What color shirt/blouse is your partner wearing? Is your partner wearing a watch? Describe your partner's shoes. What color are your partner's eyes?** Though many of us have a difficult time sharing who we really are, our appearances, speech, and actions tell others a great deal about our lives.

Discussion Questions

1. Why do we resist revealing our real selves to others?
2. What one word best describes Paul? Why?
3. How do you think Paul viewed himself? God? Others?
4. How do you feel about your level of vulnerability?
5. How can God's work be more visible through your vulnerability?
6. How can vulnerability lead to an honest relationship with others? With God?

Prayer

Ask God to help you become more vulnerable with others in your group. Thank Him for the people who have made themselves vulnerable to you.

Optional Activities

1. Ask a group member to research and report on the background of the Corinthian church, listing problems Paul dealt with in 1 Corinthians, his first letter to the church.
2. Read and report on *The Apostle: A Life of Paul* by John Pollock (Victor). Describe Paul's dedicated commitment as a follower of Christ as illustrated in this researched biography.

Assignment

1. Complete Session 2.
2. Memorize 2 Corinthians 2:14.

Session Topic: God is concerned with our attitudes toward giving as well as our giving habits.

Icebreaker
Read the following statements and determine each speaker's attitude toward giving.
- ☐ "I don't see why I have to give up my office."
- ☐ "I guess I'd better sign this get well card."
- ☐ "OK, you can borrow my lawnmower, but you better not break it."
- ☐ "Another dollar for my Christmas fund."
- ☐ "Honey, don't forget that sack for the Mission Food Pantry."
- ☐ "Take this $10 and buy more paint to finish Mrs. Jones' back porch."

Discussion Questions
1. Should giving be planned or spontaneous?
2. Do you consider yourself a generous person? What prompts you to be generous? What inhibits you?
3. For you to become more generous, what would you have to change— your time priorities? Your job? Your spending habits?
4. What are some ways that your group can be more giving to each other? To the church? To those outside the church?

Prayer
Confess any shortcomings in your attitude toward giving. Thank God for the gifts He has given you, and ask Him to help you become a generous giver.

Optional Activities
1. Review Paul's list of hardships in 2 Corinthians 6:3-10. Share some hardships you have experienced as a result of serving God.
2. Review Paul's perspective on love in 1 Corinthians 13. Then skim 2 Corinthians 6–7 for Paul's additional comments on love.

Assignment
1. Complete Session 3.
2. Memorize 2 Corinthians 9:6-7.

3

Session Topic: God develops in us healthy self-images through the thorns in our lives.

Icebreakers (*choose one*)
1. Write a short profile about yourself. Share your article with others in the group. Note whether most articles are positive or negative.
2. Evaluate your self-image by rating yourself Below Average, Average, or Above Average on the following statements:
   ❑ When it comes to physical appearance, I am. . . .
   ❑ When it comes to intelligence, I am. . . .
   ❑ When it comes to being successful and having friends, I am. . . .
   ❑ When it comes to spiritual matters, I am. . . .
   ❑ When it comes to talent, I am. . . .

Discussion Questions
1. What people make us feel inferior?
2. Why do we allow other people to control how we feel about ourselves?
3. Are other people's views of us always accurate?
4. What is the most prominent thorn or shortcoming in your life?
5. What can you do to develop trust in God during periods of weakness?

Prayer
Admit before God any shortcomings or thorns in your life. Commit to developing trust in God as you experience thorns in life.

Optional Activities
1. Keep a daily journal about your self-image for a week and then share with the group what you learned from the experience.
2. Review 2 Corinthians to determine Paul's view of authority. Ask: **How do you respond to authority? According to Paul, how should Christians exercise leadership over one another?**

Assignments
1. Complete Session 4.
2. Memorize 2 Corinthians 10:4-5.

4

Session Topic: We experience Christian freedom when we allow the Holy Spirit to produce spiritual fruit in our lives.

Icebreakers (*choose one*)
1. What is your definition of Christian freedom?
2. Read the following scenarios and discuss each character's definition of freedom. Which is closest to your own definition?
   - ❑ Mark walks up to Jim at the office Christmas party and says, "So you must think it's OK for Christians to drink. Jim responds, "I can do whatever I want whenever I want."
   - ❑ Liz invites Paula to go sailing. Paula replies, "Sorry, Liz, I checked my list of do's and don'ts. I can't do that kind of thing on a Sunday."
   - ❑ When Bob stops to change her flat tire, Mrs. Walker says, "I'm sorry you have to miss church to help me." Bob replies, "That's OK, I'm glad to be of service."

Discussion Questions
1. Read Galatians 5:13-14. What are we free from? What are we free for?
2. Have you ever seen Christian freedom abused? If so, explain.
3. How would you use the Book of Galatians to respond to those who think Christian freedom gives them license to do anything they want?
4. Have you experienced Christian freedom?

Prayer
Ask the Holy Spirit to cultivate positive fruit in your life. Pray that your Christian freedom will not become a stumbling block to others.

Optional Activities
1. Prepare an overview of the Book of Galatians. Research the Judaizers and the Council of Jerusalem.
2. Read Galatians 5:16. Rewrite the verse in your own words.

Assignment
1. Complete Session 5.
2. Memorize Galatians 5:22-23.

5

Session Topic: Goal-setting helps us out of our spiritual ruts and causes us to mature as Christians.

Icebreaker

Read the following statements and respond by agreeing or disagreeing.
- ❑ I have clear-cut goals for my future.
- ❑ A true Christian sometimes experiences disappointment, but continues to move toward his or her goals.
- ❑ Setting goals is for overachievers.
- ❑ When I fail to reach my goals, I feel down.
- ❑ I don't have to work at reaching goals; God will help me.
- ❑ I will succeed in everything if I try hard enough.
- ❑ Goals for Christlikeness are impossible to achieve.

Discussion Questions

1. What are three major concerns you have about your spiritual life now?
2. What three wishes would you make in response to your major concerns?
3. What specific plans of action can you take that will help you begin solving your spiritual concerns?

Prayer

Ask God to help you complete your plan of action. Thank Him for His work in your life.

Optional Activities

1. Prepare an overview of the Book of Ephesians. Point out that this letter was written by Paul to a congregation established on one of Paul's later missionary journeys.
2. Review the three images Paul uses in Ephesians 1:15–2:22 to describe the church: body, family, and holy temple. Ask: **In what ways are these three images similar? What are the implications of each image?**

Assignment

1. Complete Session 6.
2. Memorize Ephesians 2:8-10.

6

Session Topic: By rooting our attitudes in love, we can prevent sinful actions.

Icebreaker
Prepare a graffiti board using poster board and felt-tip markers. Write "Bad Attitude Board" in large letters at the top. Invite group members to write or draw things about which they have bad attitudes.

Discussion Questions
1. What usually happens when we display a negative attitude toward someone or something?
2. What are the sources of your negative attitudes?
3. How do you respond to others' negative attitudes?
4. Brainstorm a list of problems or difficult situations faced by Paul.
5. How would you have responded to the problems faced by Paul?
6. What sort of attitude did Paul have toward his problems?
7. What are four principles that Paul gives in Philippians for developing positive attitudes?
8. How can you apply these four principles in your own life?

Prayer
Write a short prayer of praise, focusing on who Jesus is. Add to that prayer some thanksgiving for what Jesus has done for you.

Optional Activities
1. Ask a group member to prepare an introduction to the Book of Philippians, describing conditions of the church at Philippi.
2. Review Philippians 3:12-21. Discuss the race analogy used by Paul in this passage. Ask: **Where does Paul picture himself in the race? Where do you picture yourself? What prize is Paul after? What prize are you after? How do you plan to reach your goal?**

Assignment
1. Complete Session 7.
2. Memorize Philippians 2:5-8. Review the key verses for Sessions 1–6.

7

Session Topic: God wants us to stay close to the source of truth.

Icebreakers

Read the following statements and indicate either Truth or Fiction.
- ❑ Lying is OK if it doesn't hurt anyone.
- ❑ Lying is permissible as long as you don't get caught.
- ❑ You should consider the consequences before you tell the truth.
- ❑ You can't get through life without lying.
- ❑ Some lies are worse than others.
- ❑ Sometimes you have to lie to protect a friend or family member.
- ❑ It is acceptable to tell an occasional "little white lie."
- ❑ Every successful person has had to lie at one point in his or her life to get ahead.

Discussion Questions

1. Do you always tell the truth? Why or why not?
2. Who is the most truthful person you know? How can you tell this person is honest?
3. What is one problem or issue about which you need to know the truth?
5. What actions can you take to ensure that you will know the truth about questionable issues?

Prayer

Silently commit yourself to applying what you've learned about truth.

Optional Activities

1. Ask a group member to prepare an introduction to the Book of Colossians, describing the church and city of Colosse.
2. Ask a group member to report on Gnosticism. Point out that the Gnostics claimed to have special knowledge above and beyond that of Christians. In reality, many of their beliefs contradicted biblical truth.

Assignment

1. Complete Session 8.
2. Memorize Colossians 3:17.

8

Session Topic: God wants us to anticipate rather than be fearful about Jesus' return.

Icebreaker
Read the following passages from 1 Thessalonians and describe your progress in that area as you prepare for Jesus' return: "Let us be alert and self-controlled" (5:6); "Therefore encourage one another and build each other up" (5:11); "Respect those who work hard among you, who are over you in the Lord and who admonish you" (5:12); "Live in peace with each other" (5:13); "Warn those who are idle, encourage the timid, help the weak, be patient with everyone" (5:14); "Always try to be kind to each other and to everyone else" (5:15); "Be joyful always" (5:16); "Pray continually" (5:17); "Give thanks in all circumstances" (5:18); "Do not put out the Spirit's fire" (5:19); "Do not treat prophecies with contempt" (5:20); "Test everything. Hold on to the good. Avoid every kind of evil" (5:21-22).

Discussion Questions
1. Read 1 Thessalonians 5:2-5. How do Paul's words about Jesus coming as a "thief in the night" make you feel? Why?
2. Do verses 4-5 give you any comfort? Why or why not?
3. Identify one area in which you need to make progress in preparing for Jesus' return.

Prayer
Pray for another group member as he or she works on a specific area in preparation for Jesus' return.

Optional Activities
1. Schedule a showing of the film *Thief in the Night*. This classic Christian film focuses on the Rapture and should generate some good discussion.
2. Prepare an overview of 1 Thessalonians, Paul's earliest letter.

Assignment
1. Complete Session 9.
2. Memorize 1 Thessalonians 5:9-10.

9

Session Topic: God wants us to set aside quality time for spiritual development.

Icebreakers *(choose one)*
1. List as many things or activities as possible that prevent you from using time wisely.
2. Discuss the meaning of idleness. Complete the following statement: The hardest thing for me to overcome in using my time wisely is. . . .

Discussion Questions
1. What things cause you to use your time unwisely?
2. Why does God want us to live responsibly, avoiding idleness?
3. What does idleness have to do with our relationship to Jesus Christ?
4. How can this group help you develop spiritually? By being friends? Allowing you to be open about your struggles and choices? Listening? Challenging you when you need it? Holding you to commitments?
5. What two areas would be the most difficult for you to give up or to shift to a lower priority in order to improve your spiritual development?

Prayer
Take this opportunity to ask the group's assistance in prayer for reprioritizing your life.

Optional Activities
1. Prepare a report on the themes of 2 Thessalonians.
2. Review 2 Thessalonians 2:16-17. Ask: **What two desires did Paul have for the Thessalonians? Where do you need the most encouragement and strength right now?**

Assignment
1. Complete Session 10.
2. Memorize 2 Thessalonians 2:16-17.

10

Session Topic: God wants us to recognize the potential of young people.

Icebreakers *(choose one)*
1. List as many positive things as possible about young people.
2. Describe your favorite teenager.

Discussion Questions
1. What kind of self-worth do most young people have?
2. Do you think they view themselves differently than God views them?
3. How can you share God's love with a young person?
4. Who has been a mentor to you? Describe how this person ministered to you.
5. What are some areas of your life that might have to change if you became a mentor to a young person?
6. Brainstorm ways to encourage and spiritually motivate young people.

Prayer
Thank God for the young people in your life. Ask Him for direction in setting a good example to others.

Optional Activities
1. Prepare a report on the pastoral letters of Paul (1 and 2 Timothy, Titus).
2. Review Acts 16 for background information on Timothy.
3. Study 1 Timothy 3 and list all the qualifications for spiritual leaders. Discuss the implications of each qualification as it relates to the church today.
4. Review 1 Timothy 4:12. Ask: **Have you ever been intimidated by what older people might think about you? In what ways can you demonstrate your maturity to others?**

Assignment
1. Complete Session 11.
2. Memorize 1 Timothy 4:12.

11

Session Topic: God has given us the power to overcome our timidity.

Icebreakers (*choose one*)
1. Take your "Shyness Quotient" on page 176.
2. Respond to the following statements by answering "Always," "Often," "Sometimes," or "Never."
   ❑ I feel at ease with people my own age.
   ❑ I feel at ease with young people.
   ❑ I feel at ease with older people.
   ❑ I go out of my way to make new people feel welcome.
   ❑ I look at a person when he or she is speaking to me.

Discussion Questions
1. Do other people ever interpret your shyness as snobbery?
2. What could a person do to prevent people from misinterpreting his or her shyness?
3. What are some situations in which you feel shy?
4. Brainstorm some ways that shy people can gain confidence.
5. Discuss some ways to reach out to a shy person.

Prayer
Thank God for the spirit of boldness He has given you. Ask Him for confidence in situations where you feel shy.

Optional Activities
1. Ask a teacher or professor of speech to talk to your group. Have your guest give the group some hints on how to be more confident in conversations and public speaking.
2. Obtain a copy of Lyman Coleman's *Encyclopedia of Serendipity* (Serendipity House). Try several of the group building exercises or affirmation games from the chapter titled "Communication Exercises."

Assignment
1. Complete Session 12.
2. Memorize 2 Timothy 1:7.

SHYNESS QUOTIENT

Do these statements describe you? Place a √ in the appropriate column.

Does This Describe You?	Yes	No	Sometimes
Sitting at home on a Friday night.			
Dreading to go to lunch because you'll have to sit alone.			
Looking down when you walk down a hall at work, afraid to look other people in the eye.			
Never receiving phone calls.			
Blushing whenever a person of the opposite sex speaks to you.			
Getting a tightness in your stomach as you go into the boss' office.			
Fear of dating.			
Sticking with your friends or spouse at a party.			
Letting other people do all the talking.			
Not being able to pray aloud.			
Afraid of being disliked.			
Afraid of saying something wrong.			
Feeling inferior.			
Afraid of trying new things.			
Totals			

Count the total checks in each column. If your largest total is in the **No** column, you're very friendly and outgoing; if it's in the **Sometimes** column, you're average, but you can work on being more outgoing; if it's in the **Yes** column, it's time to work at overcoming your shyness.

12

Session Topic: God wants us to forgive others because He has forgiven us.

Icebreaker
Describe the longest grudge you have ever had toward another person.

Discussion Questions
1. Are you currently holding any grudges toward others?
2. Why is it hard to forgive?
3. How do you feel when someone else won't forgive you?
4. Brainstorm some alternatives to holding grudges.
5. Which alternatives would you consider using in your life when you feel tempted to hold a grudge?

Prayer
Think of a specific person against whom you are holding a grudge. Spend some time in silent prayer using the following format:

❑ Adoration—Praise God for His love and forgiveness of your sins.

❑ Confession—Ask God to forgive you for not forgiving the person against whom you are holding a grudge.

❑ Thanksgiving—Thank God for helping you to begin overcoming your anger and resentment toward the person you chose.

❑ Supplication—Ask God to help you forgive others more readily.

Optional Activities
1. Review Titus 2. Develop a discipleship program based on Paul's teachings. Determine who is to teach whom and what is to be taught.
2. Compare the list of leadership qualifications found in 1 Timothy 3:2-7 with the list in Titus. Discuss similarities and differences.
3. Research and report on the lives of slaves in the first century. Ask: **What institutions or practices today violate basic human rights? How can we deal with these situations?**

Assignment
1. Review Sessions 1–12.
2. Review the key verses for Sessions 1–12.

REVIEW

Session Topic: God wants us to remember and apply what we've learned about Him from Paul's letters.

Choose one or two review methods, based on the size and interests of your group.

Option 1
Play "Stump the Panel." Ask several volunteers to participate on two panels. The remainder of the group should write questions about Paul's letters, trying to stump the panels with their questions. If one panel is unable to answer a question, the question is passed to their opponents. Keep score to make this competitive.

Option 2
Use the names and places found in each chapter of the text to play "Wheel of Fortune" or "Probe" with your group. New group members or members who missed several sessions will be able to participate since they merely have to choose consonants to fill in the blanks on a chalkboard or poster board. Be sure to alert each team whether the words are people, places, things, or phrases.

Option 3
Review by providing group members with the opportunity to raise questions, discuss problems, or share opinions on issues that had to be omitted during the course.

Option 4
Review the key verses from each session. Provide some sort of reward or certificate for all group members who have memorized all key verses.

·Option 5
Ask: **How has this study affected your spiritual life? Have you maintained spiritual integrity in regard to your relationship with Jesus Christ? What did you find most helpful?**

WRAP-UP

BibleLog Book 3

Please take a minute to fill out and mail this form giving us your candid reaction to this material. Thanks for your help!

1. In what setting did you use this **BibleLog** study?

If you used Book 3 for personal study only, skip to question 6.
2. How many people were in your group?

3. What was the age-range of those in your group?

4. How many weeks did you spend on this study?

5. How long was your average meeting time?

6. Did you complete the studies before discussing them with a group?

7. How long did it take you to complete the study on your own?

8. Do you plan to continue the **BibleLog** Series? Why or why not?

Would you like more information on Bible study resources for small groups?

Name _____

Address _____

Church _____

City _____ State _____ Zip _____

Adult Education Editor
Victor Books
1825 College Avenue
Wheaton, Illinois 60187